*BEAUTY IN THE FORM OF A
MYSTERIOUS GIRL OFF
THE STREETS—AND IN THE
MIND OF A GENIUS COMING
INTO HIS OWN*

Her name was Rosina. She appeared one day in Gibran's studio, told him she was a model, and calmly disrobed. Gibran found himself gazing at a vision of feminine perfection such as he had never seen in the flesh before.

For hours Gibran feverishly sketched. Hours passed unnoticed. At last Rosina said she had to leave—but not before Gibran made her promise to come again.

This was the beginning of a relationship that was to teach Gibran his ultimate lesson in the mysteries of the heart and of the soul—a relationship that cast its magic glow over—
GIBRAN IN PARIS

GIBRAN IN PARIS

by Yusuf Huwayyik

Translated and with an Introduction by Matti Moosa

POPULAR LIBRARY • NEW YORK

To my sister Fadila Moosa
with affection and gratitude

ACKNOWLEDGMENT

I wish to extend my sincere thanks to my colleague, Dr. Frank Angotti, for his innumerable editorial comments and corrections regarding the translation and the Introduction.

I would also like to express appreciation to Mrs. Charlotte Douglass whose comments and encouragement were very helpful, as well as to Mr. George Benson for his aid.

CONTENTS

PREFACE

The quotations used in the Introduction are derived mainly from the collection of Gibran's letters to Mary Haskell as well as Mary Haskell's diaries, both of which are deposited in the Archives of the University of North Carolina at Chapel Hill, North Carolina. Additional information was taken from Tawfiq Sayigh's *Adwa Jadida ala Gibran* (New Lights of Gibran) published in Arabic in Beirut in 1966 which constitutes the first thorough treatment in Arabic of Gibran's letters and Mary Haskell's diaries. A selection of these letters and diaries edited by Virginia Hilu have been published in *Beloved Prophet* (A. Knopf, 1972). Other sources include some of Gibran's published works as well as his unfinished essay *Falsafat al-Din wa al- Tadayyun* (The Philosophy of Religion and Religiosity) kept in his museum, Mikha'il Na'ima's *Khalil Gibran: Hayatuhu, Mawtuhu, Fannuhu* (Kahlil Gibran: His Life, Death, Writings and Art, Beirut, 1934), which is the first biography of Gibran in Arabic, Jamil Jabr, *Gibran: Siratuhu, Adabuhu, Falsafatuhu wa Rasmuhu* (Gibran: His Life, Writings, Philosophy and Art, Beirut, 1958) and by the same author his edition of *Rasa'il Gibran* (Gibran's Letters, Damascus, n.d.), which is a collection of some of Gibran's letters in Arabic to many of his friends and prominent Arab writers, Khalil Hawi, *Kahlil Gibran: His Background, Character and Works* (Beirut, 1963), Rose Ghurayyib, *Gibran fi Atharihi al-Kitabiyya* (Gibran From His Writings, Beirut, 1969), and Adnan Yusuf Sukayk, *al-Naz'a al-Insaniyya ind Gibran* (The

Human Tendency of Gibran, Cairo, 1970). Part of the information is based on the editor's personal interview with Gibran's close friend Mikha'il Na'ima at his home in the village of Biskanta, Lebanon, on July 6, 1972.

CONTENTS

GIBRAN IN PARIS

INTRODUCTION

☐ Kahlil Gibran has been and continues to remain a paradoxical figure both to his admirers and detractors alike. This little book, which is essentially a personal reminiscence of one of Gibran's oldest and dearest friends—Yusuf Huwayyik—while they sojourned together in Paris between the years 1909 and 1910, casts a great deal of light upon the nature of these paradoxes.

When Huwayyik met Gibran in Paris in the spring of 1909, Gibran had already made an important impact upon the Arabic world due to the appearance of his books *Nymphs of the Valleys* (1906) and *Spirits Rebellious* (1908). Huwayyik, studying art in Italy, upon hearing that Gibran was in Paris, rushed there to be with him. They had been old friends ever since their student days together in the al-Hikma school in Beirut, an institution founded and operated by the Maronites. They collaborated together on a school paper—*al-Nahda* (The Awakening)—Gibran doing most of the writing and Huwayyik acting as business manager.

Both Gibran and Huwayyik were born in the same year, 1883. Their backgrounds, however, were very different. Although both of them were Catholic Maronites, Huwayyik's family was situated in more comfortable circumstances than that of Gibran. Gibran was born in the remote village of Bsharri in northern Lebanon, the first son of the widow Kamila, daughter of a clergyman, and Khalil Sa'd Gibran, a collector of rural taxes. Huwayyik, who was born in the northern village of Hilta, came from a solid middle-class family whose distinction was enhanced by the fact that Huwayyik's uncle, Elias Huwayyik (1849-1931), was Patriarch of the Maronite church in Lebanon.

In 1894 the eleven-year-old Gibran, together with his half-brother Butrus, his mother and his two sisters, immigrated to the United States, settling on the fringes of Boston's Chinatown. It is not exactly clear why, but his father remained in Lebanon. In 1897 Gibran was sent back to Lebanon to attend school. He remained at the Hikma school until the summer of 1899 when he returned to Boston and began to make his first youthful attempts at writing and drawing. His sudden return to Boston after only two years may have been precipitated by an unhappy love affair with a wealthy young woman, Hala al-Zahir. Their disparate backrounds precluded the poor but ambitious Gibran's fulfilling his youthful ardor. The bitterness that this affair engendered was later to be described in all of its unhappy detail in his novella *The Broken Wings* (1912).

In 1902 Gibran was able to return to Lebanon once more, acting as a guide and interpreter to a wealthy American family. But this trip too was cut short, by the news that his sister Sultana had died and that his mother was seriously ill. The tragedy for Gibran, however, was not ended. His beloved half-brother, Butrus, who was the family breadwinner, soon succumbed to tuberculosis and his mother, while Gibran stood helplessly by, met the same fate in June, 1903. Gibran and his sister, Maryana, were the sole family survivors in Boston. The loss of his family, so instant and so merciless, left a shadow upon Gibran's soul and he carried it with him for the rest of his life. The impact that their death had upon him is pointedly brought out in his lament to Yusuf Huwayyik when, severely ill and believing himself about to die, he confessed through his tears and in a strained voice: "My sister, my mother, and my brother have died and I do not know what has happened to my father . . . I shall surely die before you, Yusuf."

By 1904 Gibran began to make his mark in the art circles of Boston. In January of that year Gibran held the

16

first exhibition of his paintings and drawings at the studio of Fred Holland Day, a photographer in Boston. At this exhibition his works drew the admiring attention of Mary Elizabeth Haskell, the owner and operator of the Haskell-Dean school in Boston. As a consequence, a month later she sponsored a second exhibition of his works. She was to become not only Gibran's close friend but his lifelong benefactress.

It was while paying a visit to Miss Haskell's school that he met and fell in love with one of her teachers, a beautiful young French woman, Emilie Michel, better known as Micheline. He continued to see her and their relationship became quite intimate. From his letters to Mary Haskell we know that Micheline was in Paris when Gibran was there and that they met frequently. We also know that he lived in a place close to where Micheline lived.

Huwayyik does not tell us much about Gibran's relations with women while in Paris, only that he was shy and that he was not the Don Juan that many people thought him to be. By Huwayyik's account Gibran was almost ascetic when it came to women. But Huwayyik also revealed that he was always in the company of American women. In fact, by the time he came to Paris Gibran had already had several episodes with women. His relationship with the young French teacher, Micheline, is but one instance. In a letter dated July 13, 1908, he tells Mary that Micheline was "a great help" to him. But for inexplicable reasons his attitude toward her changed. In a letter at the end of 1910, he reveals: "Poor Micheline! I do not have anything to say to her. But she is very dear to me, and I constantly pray that she will find a good man." And again in the spring of 1911 he tells Mary, "Poor Micheline! The gods of hell yell to her and she cannot block her ears." There is no doubt that at this time he kept from Mary Haskell the real nature of his relationship with Micheline. He spoke always in general terms about her in his letters. It was only gradually that he revealed to Mary the nature of his true past relations with Micheline: as for instance in 1912 he says,

17

"In her there is something certain, something real which I neglected to see years ago when I was to a great extent a poet and to a lesser extent a man." And finally in 1914 he fully confesses to her, speaking of his "childish behavior" and that "I and Micheline had very intimate relations." Furthermore, two years earlier, in 1912, he had told Mary that, contrary to popular belief, he had several intimate relationships during the past few years. In an outburst of uncharacteristic candor he was anxious to tell her how many times and with whom he had sexual relations, but she rebuffed him, refusing to hear about them.

Gibran's relationship with Mary Haskell was, considered altogether, rather strange. Ten years older than he, this strait-laced American woman had not only been drawn to his talent but also to his dark and sensitive, almost exotic looks. Even though she later confessed to him her latent lesbianism, her diaries reveal that she and Gibran had many times made love, stopping just short of its final and logical consummation. She confessed, rather unconvincingly, that they were afraid of people's gossip and most of all pregnancy.

In 1906 Gibran published his first important work, *Nymphs of the Valley*, a collection of short stories which, taken together, added up to a scathing attack against institutionalized religion and the outmoded traditions and laws of Eastern society. Although he does not really deserve the label, this book branded him as being a sort of revolutionary.

The role of rebel was to be further played in *Spirits Rebellious* which he published in 1908. Dedicated to Micheline, this latter work of the young "revolutionary" attacks the marriage customs and the unfortunate situation of women in the Middle East. But he does not offer any concrete palliatives as a substitution for indulgent invective. In the same year in which *Spirits Rebellious* was published, Gibran left for Paris. He was able to do so through the great generosity of Mary Haskell who believed that Gibran was worth investing in. He had convinced her that by going to Paris he would be better able to achieve his ambition of being a first-rate artist and writer.

At this time, he had either begun writing his novella *The Broken Wings* or had finished its first draft. The implication that one gets from the diaries of Mary Haskell is that it was more likely the latter. This romance appeared in 1912. In the meantime, he had been working on several essays which he finished in Paris and which were published in 1914 under the title *A Tear and a Smile*. In a letter written from Paris to Mary Haskell in early 1909 we have a clue as to what Gibran was seeking there: "Both of us", he writes, speaking of himself and Huwayyik, "endeavor to do something but in different ways. My friend searches for himself in nature while I search for myself through nature. Art to me is higher than the things we see and hear. Nature is nothing but the body of God, the form of God and it is God whom I am seeking and would like to understand." The central idea of Gibran, that we can find God or higher reality in nature and identify ourselves through it, finds its roots in the interaction of romanticism with the philosophy of Kant. It was in the latter's philosophy that this pantheistic sense of spirit in nature received explicit formulation.

By this time Gibran had read and been influenced by the Romantics, including Blake, Wordsworth, Rousseau and the Americans Thoreau and Emerson; it was through them that he was influenced by the realism of Kant. Gibran had deep-felt romantic roots. In an age of the rising supremacy of symbolism and naturalism in literature he betrays his Arabic roots and basic alienation by his attachment to an "unstylish" romanticism epitomized by his belief that one can see God or higher reality in nature, commune with it and be reborn through it. The Romantics believed that it was the artist, the poet who feels the infinite spirit in him when he creates and it is intuition that yields a much deeper truth than that to be found on the rational and analytical plane. Gibran had remarked, "I am the maker of symbols," but his poetic images are all symbols of nature, which is for him truly the key to reality, the reality of self and God.

William Blake influenced him deeply. Indeed, he once said that "Blake is the god-man . . . his vision . . . is the most godly." The visionary-religious element in romanticism was epitomized by the works of Blake, the English artist-poet-mystic. The spiritual parallels between Gibran and Blake are too strong not to be taken seriously. Blake had believed in the identification of his own thought with the soul of the universe. Like Gibran, later on, especially in *The Prophet*, he believed that it was the mission of the poet and artist to be a religious prophet.

Some Arab writers have misunderstood the true essence of the romantic strain in Gibran. While the question has puzzled a great many people for some time it can be more or less safely stated that romanticism's basic criteria were at least the following: expression of the emotions, love of nature, intuition as truth and a revolt against what was deemed to be the restraints and strictures of a society that enchained the spirit. Romanticism began, of course, as a reaction against the eighteenth century, with its overt rationalism and continuing obeisance to classicism. Reason was to be replaced by the emotive and intuitive springs of human creativity. This was the heart of romanticism. Within Gibran there was a juxtaposition of the formal aspects of both negative and positive romanticism. Again and again Huwayyik reveals Gibran in revolt against arid formalism, especially that of the Arabic literary world. It was Gibran who first broke the constraining bonds of an empty and arid Arabic classicism, with its emphasis on form and tradition, and opened the way for modern Arab writers.

A positive emphasis upon the imagination, the aesthetic, and the mystery and terror of life approached through the subjective and the intuitive was the other side of the coin. It cannot be over-emphasized that subjectivism, which was an essential part of the romantic movement, was also one of the mainsprings of Gibran's creative position. His Western mind saw that the Arabic position of looking upon the mind as being eternally passive, a lazy onlooker of the external world, robbed them of that assertive force necessary for progress and creativity. The Arab system to him was inherently false because, like the romantics, he believed that any society based upon passivity of mind and a religion-based rejection of anything that was different was weak, and false because weak. This positive assertion of self and life was one of the central doctrines of the romantics derived in great part from Kant, and it has left its stamp on the contemporary Western world. This energetic, affirmative, forceful approach to oneself and the external world which we call subjectivism is, perhaps, the leading theme of the West. This attitude, which one must understand in order to understand Gibran, is manifest in all of his works: a romantic conception of the free individual, an individual freed from all external restraint because man and man alone is the creator of his own genius, the designer of his fate. This emphasis upon the individual is a foreign concept to the Arabic world—a world unequivocally sentimental and emotional, lacking the necessary philosophical, intellectual, and religious antecedents to mold it into effective and positive channels of creation and life. This is why Gibran's works were never fully understood in the East.

Gibran, however, even though in many ways a Westerner, was somewhat of an anachronism in the West. In spite of what we have just said, his heart, at least in his earlier sentimental state, was Arabic. He had been born in Lebanon, he received the only higher education he was ever to get in Lebanon and he lived within the cultural milieu of the Syrian community in the United States. Anyone who is acquainted with the religio-historical ethos of the Arab world can grasp much of what this meant. The Arabs are a sentimentalized people with the individual immersed in a cultural unity more metaphysical than political, which lends itself to a collective languor and "romantic" conception of life with connotations and ramifications different than that of Western society. Thus, due to their historical and geographical, but most of all, their religious and social traditions, there has been produced a result which can only be described as an exaggerated conception of life. Gibran, as part of

21

this and romanticism, was drawn to out-moded themes, sentimental exaggerations, to an at times immature and almost embarrassing emotionalism. While much of his unique Arabism remained with him until the end of his days, soon after he left Paris, when he had begun to come under the influence of Nietzsche, he began to change.

It is at this time that we catch a glimpse of the beginning of a rather subtle but nonetheless inexorable transmogrification of Gibran from Eastern to Western man. The signal for this was sounded by his early adoption and adaptation of Nietzsche's philosophy. In a letter to Mary Haskell in 1911 he made a revealing confession: "At first I used to be a man of highly emotional sympathy; I championed the underdog. I wet myself with tears and lamentation. But this is the way of the East. The East is effete and I despise it. It stands for everything that is decadent and crude."

In Chapter Fifteen he adopts the typically Nietzschean stand in relation to the subject of love. Huwayyik tells us how Gibran rebuked him after he spoke of love as spiritual beauty. Gibran laughingly chided him, "It's spiritual beauty? You talk like one of the Sisters of Charity. It seems to me that there are still within you traces of priestly influence." To him love had become almost a purely physical thing, a matter of domination and superiority. While he did not immediately begin to adopt a strictly Western approach and idiom to express his ideas, the few remaining (and unimportant) works which he wrote in Arabic were influenced by his changing attitude and position. The Nietzschean ideas of the will to power, the concept of the superman and the relativism of morality began to make their appearance in one form or another.

The final signal that the transmogrification had been completed was when his most important work from a personal as well as objective standpoint—*The Prophet* (1923)—was published in English. Gibran never again dealt with purely Eastern themes although he still remained in love with Eastern literary forms, i.e., the parable, the aphorism, the metaphor and the didactic moral lesson. He had totally rejected "redemption" through Eastern philosophy and thought.

The nature of Nietzsche's influence upon Gibran has been pointed out by various writers, but it has usually been misunderstood. We have already spoken of Gibran's change from a "man of many tears" to a man more assertive towards life and less sympathetic to what he considered the weakness and uncertainty of others. Soon after coming to Paris, and all during that time, increasingly he came under the influence of Nietzsche. "What I felt five years ago," he wrote in 1911 to Mary Haskell, "I no longer feel today. However, I do not want to throw it away." He was referring to his book, *The Broken Wings*, which was no longer reflective of his true attitude. The life of emotion was beginning to give way to the Nietzschean will to power. An insight into the influence of Nietzsche at this time can be found in his answer to the question he asks in Chapter Eight: "Who are we?" This was to be a recurring question for Gibran. He would ask it again and again to the end of his life. But since he rejected the Biblical concept of the idea of man made in God's image who, redeemed through Christ, will one day return to God, he sought to explain this question in purely secular terms.

This rejection probably lies behind the idea of reincarnation which keeps cropping up in his works and this idea was strengthened by the doctrine of the eternal recurrence found in the works of Nietzsche, a theory geared to the affirmation of life in man's personal and persistent relationship to it. This humanistic approach is that of *The Prophet* which is a book closely parallel to the form and spirit of *Thus Spake Zarathustra*.

It was in 1913 that Gibran told Mary Haskell that "Nietzsche took the words out of my mouth." He was angry because in *Thus Spake Zarathustra* he had found many of the things that he wanted to say in the way he would have wanted to say them. The Nietzchean influence upon *The Prophet* is significantly manifest in the assertion made in this latter work that man achieves redemption not through divine revelation but rather gives a divine aspect to his life by adhering to the word of the guiding Prophet. Like Schopenhauer before him Nietzsche had depicted life as terrible and tragic, speaking of its redemption through art and the work of creative genius. This is not far removed from the spirit that lies behind *The Prophet*. There is a commensurate assent in both Nietzsche's and Gibran's work in the affirmation of life rather than its negation. This is true, despite the fact that Nietzsche's early attitude, like Gibran's, was rather negative. He was bitter and alienated against much of what he saw in contemporary civilization. However negative Gibran himself was, as soon as he came under Nietzschean philosophy he began to turn like Nietzsche toward a powerful affirmation of life rather than toward its negation, and he did so in a way that paralleled both the spirit and terminology of Nietzsche.

Nietzsche relates in his book, *The Birth of Tragedy*, that life is terrible, inexplicable, and dangerous. But even though one is alive to the real character of the world and of human life one does not surrender to pessimism by turning his back on life. What was necessary was to transmute the world and human life through art and affirm the world as an aesthetic phenomenon. There were two ways of achieving this positive attitude and they corresponded respectively to the Dionysian and Apollonian attitudes or mentalities. Dionysus is for Nietzsche the symbol of the stream of life, which breaks down all barriers and ignores all restraints. Man is intoxicated, as it were, with the will to life and power. But Gibran did not follow this particular path. Rather he follows the Nietzschean mode of the Apollonian approach to life by which one draws an aesthetic veil over reality creating an ideal world of form and beauty. In many times and in many places Gibran had said, "I am the maker of forms, I am the maker of symbols," and in doing so he was striving for the unique and ideal. This was an ideal that he believed should be reflected in the work, the attitudes and the life of man. We find in *The Prophet* the optimistic, almost mystical, belief of Nietzsche that the human being, with his infinitely adaptive and mobile nature, has a great capacity for self-transcendence and the realization of fresh possibilities. In order to do this, however, he needs a clearly defined and consistent goal, a sense of direction as it were. Empirical science is incapable of giving this goal or direction to man. And though Nietzsche himself does not have much to say about Christianity, he does look to religion as the source of the requisite vision. Hence, the creation of *Thus Spake Zarathustra*.

The philosophy of *The Prophet*, in like manner, is not represented by the learned scientists and professors of the day but by the lonely thinker, Zarathustra, or, if you wish, al-Mustafa, who has a clear vision of the possibilities of man's self transcendence. The message behind *The Prophet* is that one should set himself with ruthless courage to the task of improving those aspects of the world which are susceptible to change with the overriding goal of self-fulfillment through the transcendence of self.

But the key phrase in order to understand the intimate nexus between Nietzsche and Gibran and the ultimate instrument of self-fulfillment is the will to power. This simply means that the world is, in truth, a metaphysical unity which transcends the self and it is the will to power that imposes upon it an intelligible character. This theory is an interpretation of the universe, a way of looking at it and describing it—a sort of *weltanschauung* of method and meaning and not a metaphysical doctrine about a metaphysical reality which lies behind the "door" of the visible world.

In the works of Gibran, which often reflect this doctrine, the essence of what Nietzsche meant has been, for the most part, missed and the purely superficial and emotive aspects of the theory are emphasized. The will to power and the will to life appear in many of Gibran's writings but most especially in the collections of stories and essays entitled *The Tempests* (1915), which is also the signal for a more pronounced change in his point of view vis-à-vis the Arabic East. In this collection he pours invective and anger upon his own people calling them "sons of monkeys", "grandsons of monkeys", and "crucified Jesuses" because they are "weak, fearful and passive". Nietzsche was less crude and affirmed that life must be challenged through the will to power that overcomes one's weakness in the face of the great flux. In his essays, *Sons of the Gods* (1917), Gibran reveals that he no longer pities nor sympathizes with weakness but rather despises it because weakness hampers the development of life and stands in the way of man's total affirmation of it as a unique individual who achieves mastery of world and self and, therefore, freedom through a constant struggle against and continual overcoming of the handicaps that are placed in his path. In his essay *Mighty Men* (1919), we can see a further elaboration upon this doctrine and the impact of Darwin through Nietzsche upon Gibran through his adaptation of the idea of "survival of the fittest." In this work he is completely transfigured. He no longer quails at the thought of war and is no longer meek in the face of adversity. He welcomes struggle, and the result of this struggle, as he perceives it, is that weakness and the weak will perish. This is good.

There are echoes in all this of Nietzsche's *Beyond Good and Evil* in which he discovered two primary texts of morality: the master morality and the slave morality. In civilization they are mixed, but one must distinguish between them. In the master morality or the aristocratic morality, good and bad are equivalent to noble and despicable. The slave morality is the standard of the weak and the powerless society. Qualities such as sympathy, kindness and humility are, in this type of society, extolled as virtues while, at the same time, in a society such as this, the strong and independent are regarded as dangerous and, therefore, as evil. Accordingly, by the standards of slave morality the good man of the master morality tends to be equated with evil. Slave morality is the morality of the sheepish masses; it is that of Christianity, the collective values of which express the needs of the herd. The higher type of man doesn't need this, he creates values out of the abundance of his life and strength. The herd, however, fears the strong and the powerful and attempts to curb and tame them by asserting as absolute their feral

26

values. There are, although hardly as intelligent, consistent echoes of the master morality vis-à-vis slave morality in the works of Gibran after 1912.

Even Jesus, whom Gibran admired, was no longer pictured by him as meek, submissive and mild but as a mighty personage, one whose strength and assertive qualities in the face of life was withal the essence of the "superman". In *The Grave Digger*, an essay published in 1920 and strongly reflective of his changed state of mind, Gibran declared that marriage, children and country are handicaps which impede man's progress, and "delay" his fulfillment as "superman". He speaks of "good and evil" and urges an overcoming of the so-called "herd morality" which, in his opinion, ensures mediocrity and breeds boredom. In *The Grave Digger*, Gibran views all human values as imminent in man, and that belief in God, the honor afforded the prophets, the emphasis placed upon religious values and the hope of heavenly estates are hollow acts devoid of meaning, invented and perpetuated by men.

Nietzsche does not go so far. He does not mean to imply in his phrase "standing above good and evil" that all respect for human values should be abandoned and all self restraint thrown overboard. The man who completely ignores the restraints of social morality may be himself so weak and degenerate that he renders himself useless. It is only the unique individual who can safely go "beyond good and evil" in the sense which these terms bear. And he does so in order to create values which will be both an expression of progressive existence and a vehicle for man to transcend himself in the direction of a superman—in short, to attain a higher level of human life.

In *The Grave Digger* Gibran does, in a way, attempt to express this ideal when he writes, "The abstract truth, however, is that you believe in and honor yourself. Do not follow anyone or believe anything except your own immortality. From the beginning man has repeated himself under different names and guises which reflect his tendencies, which reflect his expectations, which reflect his destiny."

27

Nietzsche had insisted that knowledge is an instrument of power whose aim is not to know in the sense of grasping absolute truth for its own sake but to master life. Human beings seek, always and everywhere, to impose order and form upon the myriad of impressions and sensations that comprise an essential part of their individual and collective existence. Reality is becoming, and we turn it into relevant being by the imposition of stable patterns and the idea of becoming. This activity carried to its higher degrees is the expression of the "will to power". It was as an impetus for the fulfillment of the potentially higher man that Nietzsche devised the myth of the superman. Man, he wrote, must be surpassed and, as such, man is a bridge and not a goal. In *Thus Spake Zarathustra*, a book that left a very strong imprint on the mind of Gibran, he said, "Man is a rope stretched between animal and superman, a rope over an abyss." But it is not simply a question of man evolving into superman, nor is it a process of "survival of the fittest". Superman cannot appear unless certain superior individuals have the courage to "transvalue all values", to break out of the constraining bonds of values, especially Christian values, and create new ones out of a super-abundant existence and strength. *The Prophet*, Kahlil Gibran's most famous work and the one which he considered most worthwhile, seeks to do just this. It is the new values as advocated by the Prophet, al-Mustafa, that give direction to the efforts and determine the goals of the higher man—"superman".

Nevertheless, while Gibran was in Paris, Huwayyik reveals that Gibran was under the influence of a state of mind which the former coined as "Franciscanism". He meant that Gibran, in his youthful and romantic psyche, combined elements of mysticism with a sympathetic attitude toward those whom he considered the oppressed and the weak. His ultimate concern was to reform the world which, for the time being, would have to wait. At this time, it was the Arabic world upon which he focused and which he wanted to enlighten, emancipate and enliven. Such a position had already been taken in Gibran's previously published works, as for instance, *Warda*

28

al-Hani, *The Bride's Bed*, and his novella, *The Broken Wings*; they reverberate with Gibran's outraged protest against marriages based not upon free choice and love but upon socio-economic grounds. Superficially and monotonously he portrays an archetypal woman: poor, beautiful but helpless, who is forced to marry a much older rich man whom she does not love. The stories always end in either the woman leaving her husband in an audacious revolt against the harsh impositions of her society to live with a young man she loves or, her spirit shrivels and she dies lamenting the unkind hand of fate. In *Warda al-Hani*, for instance, the heroine, caught between two imperatives, love and duty, obeys what appears to her to be the higher and more noble calling— love, even though it condemns her to a life of wretched poverty. She makes a free and individual choice implicitly condemning the passive acceptance of historical social custom.

In all of these earlier works, Gibran portrays woman as the victim of a stagnant, rigid and cruel tradition. He burns with indignation and tells Huwayyik that most people wallow in a maelstrom of lies, traditions, and outworn customs but, "I am the enemy of their hypocrisy and duplicity. I shall tell them this in order to shame them."

Most of these earlier stories are also highly critical of priests and institutionalized religion, and the laws surrounding them. He sees them as being partly to blame for the misery of the Eastern woman since it is their laws that legalize her ties with a man whom she does not love. He bitterly denounces priests for having made laws based on ignorance and injustice. The poor woman married to a man she hates had, Gibran maintains, never been consulted by the priests when they made these laws. Furthermore, these laws, he emphasizes, are far removed from divine justice and the God to whom the priests attribute their origin. Gibran seems to believe that a true marriage is one based on mutual love between free spirits, not one sanctioned by priestly laws. No better expression of this idea can be found than in the words of his rebellious heroine, Warda al-Hani, who, caught in the grip of an intolerable marriage to an old and rich man, went to live with her lover; she describes her plight thus:

> When I awakened to the dead weight of my wings which were incapable of lifting me to the heaven, love, because of the tethers of religious laws, I understood at last the essence of those laws. I came to realize that happiness is not to be found in wealth or social prestige but in love which makes of man and woman one member of the body of life and one word on the lips of God.

But Gibran does not really tell all, vitiated as his understanding is by a somewhat spurious naiveté. His vehement attack against religious laws and the priests whom he claims have enacted them is unwarranted. Gibran overlooked the fact that religious law in the Middle East, whether Christian or Muslim, was bound to bless marriages regardless of the ages and love relationship between the partners. The priests who execute these laws do not by doing so personally sanction the marriage but merely do their duty. They are not quite the villains which Gibran portrays them as being. The Easterner and particularly the Arab woman have been burdened by the weight of ancient socio-economic factors and distinctions which have inextricably woven a web of inequality and degradation into their lives. It is not the priestly laws that have done this. Woman has been secluded and dictated to for generations, a situation that finds its roots in the values and mores of a long-forgotten age and the constant selfishness of men. Many women in the Middle East, even today, still remember the saying, "Woman is made either for man or the grave."

Certainly, Gibran knew about these socio-economic and historical factors and he was right in attacking them and decrying them with all the literary force that he could muster. At the same time the priests certainly were not always the paragons of virtue in that society and he rightly denounced their sometimes callous and unconcerned attitude toward some of the most elementary principles of justice and charity. This is amply and forcefully brought out in his two completely anti-clerical stories, *John the Madman* and *Khalil the Heretic*.

But Gibran does sometimes recognize more factors as being involved in the unjust state of marriage in the East than those which could be attributed to priests. For instance, Sulma Karama, the protagonist of *The Broken Wings*, is presented as only partially the victim of religious law or priestly arrogance. Coming from a prestigious and wealthy family, she fell deeply in love with a young man of rather unstable circumstances. Only eighteen years old, he had no financial resources nor even a goal in life. In the nineteenth century (and indeed, even today) it was literally impossible for a man to consider marriage without a job or sufficient resources. If Gibran rails against this unfortunate truism, he also must have known that love in the Arab world was far from being the only secure basis for a successful marriage. Even today, Middle Easterners frown upon early marriages since, without a job, a home and the ability to meet family obligations, marriage can become an evil institution.

But Gibran, young romanticist that he was, could not really tackle the problem of forced or fixed marriages and defend the rights of Eastern woman except through highly sentimental pathos. Besides, Gibran was not the first to champion the rights of women in the Arab world. Several decades before, a group of writers in Syria and Egypt had protested against injustice done to women and called not only for their right to marry the man of their choice but the quality of their education as well. Among these writers are As'ad Ya'qub Khayyat, the celebrated Butrus al-Bustani (who delivered a speech on behalf of woman's rights before the Syrian Scientific Society as early as 1849), his son Salim al-Bustani (d. 1884), Adib Ishaw (d. 1885), Faris al-Shidyaq (d. 1888), Francis Marrash (d. 1873), and the greatest champion of women's rights in Egypt, Qasim Amin (d. 1908). Nu'man Abduh al-Qasatli (d. 1920) also published many stories in al-

Bustani's periodical, *al-Jinan*, which vividly portrayed not only the sad plight of women but also protested against cruel social and economic traditions.

Yet, despite Gibran's rather particularist concerns and youthful naiveté, this little book, along with many of the letters to Mary Haskell during this Paris sojourn, reveals to us that Gibran had in his makeup many of the elements and attitudes which would go into and be manifested in the later *Prophet*. Certainly this book reveals to us that he took the position of being the superior, teacher, and guide of those around him. He tried by both word and deed to set an example not only for Huwayyik but for the various other characters that come into play. His ego would not let him be content with a sharing of viewpoints and ideas. He believed himself and himself alone to be in communication with the truth—a gift given only rarely to unique individuals. There is little room for doubt that he regarded himself—even at this time—as this unique individual.

In fact, in 1911 he wrote to Mary Haskell that Yusuf Huwayyik was "his boy" when they were together at the Hikma school in Beirut and that he and he alone had taken the responsibility to inspire him and instruct him. He tells her, furthermore, that in Paris Gibran was the source of the development and growth of Huwayyik's talent. Mary wrote back asking Gibran if Huwayyik was his best friend, or whether this honor befell someone else. Gibran wrote back that there was no such a person but that Huwayyik would, perhaps, most nearly fit the description of best friend. In a later letter, Mary asked whether or not Gibran was older than Huwayyik. Although he well knew that they were the same age, nevertheless, Gibran replied that he has always felt like the spiritual father of Huwayyik, and that while they were in Beirut and now in Paris, he considered him as a spiritual son. It had been he alone who was responsible for teaching Huwayyik to draw; he had inspired him and was the father of his destiny.

In another place he tells Mary that "Yusuf thought I was astonishing because I could draw a tree or a cat." He portrays Huwayyik as very shy, so shy in fact that whenever he wrote or drew something he never allowed anyone to see it except Gibran. Of course the witness born by Huwayyik challenges the truth of this statement. Huwayyik has absolutely no hesitation in bringing Calmie, a relative stranger, to his room; he has no hesitation in passing out to his coffee house companions the drawings which he had made at the art academy. And, indeed, it is he and not Gibran who makes many friends with whom he has a grand time; he talks with them, jokes with them, visits with them and enjoys their circle of banter, conversation and wit at the Café Dôme.

But Gibran is truly fond of Huwayyik and he writes in a letter of 1911: "This young man is really astonishing. I believe that he loves what is best. He is like a slow fire, very slow. But a fire which will some day erupt, perhaps into a volcano. I love him tremendously. It's perhaps selfish of me because in a sense he is my pupil." Thus Gibran again reveals the attitude of the teacher and the prophet. While Huwayyik does not give us much evidence as to the real truth of this "father-son", teacher-student, leader-follower relationship, perhaps there is an element of truth in it. Most certainly it was not exactly the situation and relationship that Gibran related to Mary Haskell. Huwayyik has respect for Gibran, he listens to him, but he does not always agree with him and, indeed, argues with and sometimes even chastises him—especially when Gibran indulges in ideas that he believes to be childish, ridiculous or unrealistic.

In 1912 Gibran wrote, in another letter to Mary Haskell, that Huwayyik did not know how to go about doing many things. However, he liked all that he did do and was attracted to Huwayyik even more when he did not do a good job. In this lies an insight into the makeup of Gibran's mental state at this time, into something that was to be manifest for the rest of his life. "When he does not really do a good job"—here is the key phrase. Huwayyik, not being completely independent and perfect, "needs" Gibran to play the mentor, the teacher, the spiritual prophet, the one who encourages, the one who says,

"Follow me," the one who always and everywhere may and must assume the role of instructor and that of him who knows best. Gibran seems to have really believed in this picture of himself. There is evidence that this self-assured role was tolerated.

Huwayyik reveals to us Gibran's ambition and, in its frustration, his dissatisfaction with himself and the world. Yet he also tells us that he was gentle, kind and shy and that he behaved with great deportment. He was actually loved by those who knew him. Olga, a refined and intelligent young woman whom we are introduced to in the first chapter, liked Gibran and admired his ambition. She was fascinated by what, for lack of a better word, could only be called his charisma, especially when he talked. Obviously Gibran achieved the correct impression with her that he was trying to create because she told Huwayyik that it seemed to her she could see something like a halo over his head. The simple and uneducated Italian model Rosina, however, did not understand Gibran. Nevertheless, she described him as a "prince" in what seemed to her the best word to describe his aristocratic behavior.

That Gibran was at times intolerant and dogmatic was not always manifest to his friends and close associates. Gibran exclaims in chapter two that he wishes to "shame" his fellow men and teach them the error of their ways. Can he have perhaps been thinking that he was truly destined to be *the* prophet and teacher of men? It seems so. He shows himself as a man who has already come to the conclusion, however mysteriously, that the truth and he are somehow in a mystical union with the divine.

Gibran's view of the artist is intimately tied up with and related to his egotistic stance as prophet and "guiding father". The artist to him is somehow a unique being —a being such as himself. A person who gleans the unusual from the usual and whose understanding is somehow deeper. The rest of humanity lacks the soul or the vision of the artist and, therefore, is relegated to the status of "shadows" on both sides of the bright "boule-

34

vards of life". It is to the artist, the artist epitomized as poet, prophet and teacher, that we must turn in order to be enlightened and transmute those insubstantial shadows of self into something more bright and shining, concrete and real.

He wrote in 1911 to Mary Haskell:

I know that I have something to tell to the world; something different from anyone else. It seems that even now I have succeeded in accomplishing something, however small it is. I have, however, made more difficult my happiness; for when I fail I become miserably unhappy and then I tell myself how much of a fool I was to have felt happy even for an instant. But then once again happiness envelopes me and I tell myself what a fool I was to have felt unhappy . . . I am certain that if I die tomorrow some of what I have said will survive. However there is nothing in all that I have accomplished which pleases me even for a short while after I have finished . . . I feel disgusted when I read what I have written because I had wanted to say it in a different manner, and I thought that it could have been said in a different manner but it does not come out that way. Sometimes my torment becomes so great that I even burst into tears. I cannot escape tears.

Other letters written around the same time reveal that Gibran's attitude toward his work and toward his critics was not consistent. For instance, he had written in a letter of 1910, "Critics in the East say many cruel things about me such as I am a destroyer of morals and that I live in the shadow of a strange god. Such criticism does not bother me, however. Indeed, I enjoy it." And later, early in 1911, he wrote that the "Arab journals write about me more than anyone else in the Arab world. But I do not read half of what has been written. Indeed I don't even read what the critics say about me in most cases." The eyes of the Arab world, it seemed, watched him with interest. He tells Mary that a newspaper published a caricature of him riding a donkey with his face toward the back of the beast, surrounded by his supporters, the "Gibranists", hailing his triumphant entry into Damascus. It was amusing, he thought, and he did not become very upset over it.

But in 1912 he once again changed his mind and took himself more seriously; "I believe, Mary," he wrote, "that the future will not be too harsh to me." And he goes on to affirm that because of his writings, "there will be some people who can free themselves from all of yesterday's bonds. Those who can endure life in the present time are relatively few but they are the strongest of all. If I can open a place in man's heart then I will not have lived in vain."

These words of Gibran might seem strange until we remember his melancholy and youthful romanticism which, a priori, assigned most people to an existence of painful endurance. He considered himself, of course, as one of those who, enduring life, are among the strongest of all. But the paradox in all this is that Gibran never really understood or assimilated his own time. He never really understood modern civilization and as such was never part of modern life. He lived on the periphery of reality in his own world of individual fantasy and intellectual isolation. He was a man estranged not only from his own times but, the greatest irony of all, from most of those people "out there" whom he thought to teach. He is typically vague in his statement about wishing to "open a place in man's heart". What does he mean by this place? Does he mean a place where Gibran's words of solace and comfort can repose, or does he mean man looking upon himself and in understanding the "I" affirms the love of the "other"? Whatever he meant, there can be no doubt that Gibran wanted to be loved.

As early as 1909 he had written to Mary, "I want to be loved and worshiped for generations!" Encouraging Gibran in his illusions and self-glorification, she constantly assured him in her replies that he was as great as Christ, great as Buddha, Shakespeare, Michaelangelo, and others. In a 1916 letter to his benefactress he made another revelatory statement: "Do you know, Mary, how happy I become when I hear the people praise my writing? But that praise also makes me very sad because . . . I want to be loved for the things which I have not yet done." In the same letter he concludes by telling Mary that, "In Syria they call me 'The Gravedigger', which I am. I love to be called this, because I dig my own grave." What Gibran means by this is uncertain—perhaps not even he knew the real meaning of this statement; certainly to the literal-minded Westerner it means absolutely nothing.

A self-admitted "creator of forms", he encapsulated his own structured and mediocre thought in the elastic symbols of the East. But in doing so he alienated those whom he wished most to reach, and those he did impress —as he more than once lamented—were the ones who needed him the least.

Gibran's ego, or perhaps, more correctly, his self-assumed role and image of himself as leader and teacher, precluded his telling people of his true origins, his real background; indeed, he was so anxious to maintain his image that he sometimes lied. Huwayyik reveals that on the event of their friend Calmie's marriage, Gibran tells a far-fetched story about his grandfather, Gibran portraying him as having been a soldier of courage and strength, a man of influence and power. In truth, his ancestors were poor and illiterate, undistinguished except by the lack of any great distinction. Furthermore, during his stay in Paris, he wrote to Mary of the richness of his family, the educated grace of his mother, the distinguished culture of his father. Their village hovel became a mansion and his obscure ancestors became ancient and honorable governors of Lebanon during the Christian Crusades. One of them, so Gibran tells it, had even attempted to inspire the European powers to a new crusade, but alas, through no fault of his own, he had failed. Earlier he had told her that he had received the scar on his arm while leading a riot in Paris against the Turks in 1911. In the autumn of 1928 he told her that he had not bothered to respond to the pleas of his countrymen to come to Lebanon and govern them. This was, of course, pure fabrication on his part. All of these instances (and there are more in a similar vein) are reflective of his need to be recognized and the confusion in his psyche of the valid borders between the external and the objective and the internal and the subjective. The distinction between wish and reality was blurred. Perhaps he thought by verbalizing these and other grand things about himself that he was by no means an ordinary being. It also reveals that Gibran was not really interested in being considered poor or humble, and even less interested in living a life of humility and poverty. "Blessed are the poor" was a truism that was valid only in its relation to others. In his attempt to give wealth and power to his parents and in manifesting a princely attitude toward waitresses and other people in Paris, he wished to demonstrate that he was no commoner, but a man to be respected, a man who, for his noble lineage and princely bearing, deserved to be admired and trusted.

If Gibran was, at this time, not greatly concerned with living a life of Christian humility, he was taken up with the subject of religion in general and particularly the origins of religion. He explains to Huwayyik (chapter Seven) that he is planning to write a book "about religion and religiosity" and expects that this book will create a great stir. This work, however, was never completed. What's more, where Gibran has written about religion he does not approach it like a scholar but like a visionary. For instance, speaking through his protagonist, Khalil the son of Salim, he tried to prove that one can communicate directly with God without the aid of organized religion, the intercession of priests, or the existence of places of worship. Hence, Khalil prays in the open, in the wilderness, where, in facing nature, he faces God. Nor for him the restricting atmosphere of church or temple. God has to be sought in the beauty of nature; the singing of birds, the rippling of streams, the waving fields of ripened wheat, all of these are more appropriate to the throne of the spirit, implies Gibran, than churches and temples.

Religion, he maintains, is One and springs from a com-

38

mon source. It has been fragmented because men have sought in various times and places to turn it to the service of their own interest and viewpoints. It is, in fact, the temple of nature that redeems man. In worshipping nature man faces himself because he is a part of nature and therefore, God. Man is the self-reflective and creative being of nature. He and he alone understands with an act of conscious reflection his place in the meaning of God.

In this sense, Khalil believed in the divinity of great men and especially Christ. He also believed in the teachings of Moses, Buddha, Confucius and other great sages of the past. He believed that they have all enlightened people and brought about the greater perfection of man and, in this, the greater perfection of God. Gibran did not believe that Jesus was divine and, indeed, in his later work, *Jesus, the Son of Man*, we see him as a human sage, cast more in the mold of Superman than savior. God is nature, and man's spirit, as the highest embodiment of that nature, makes God more perfect in his increasingly self-conscious realization. This is all quite vague and very Hegelian, but without the historical acumen and intelligent philosophical insight of Hegel.

Gibran seems early to have abandoned any allegiance to institutionalized religion in favor of the belief that religion is nothing more than an individual experience, a mystical exercise between man and the God who is everywhere. The only ritual that is needed is the ritual of assent to the beauty of nature and the ubiquitous presence of God as a kind of transcendent eminence in that nature. In *Iram, the City of Lofty Pillars* (1921), Gibran expresses the idea of the abstract essence of life when he proclaims that "everything in existence exists within man, everything that is within man exists in existence. There is no boundary between the near and far, the high and low, the big and the small. It is one." Furthermore, one cannot see oneself in the totality of life, except through an exercise of transcendence which Gibran calls "the ultimate desire" which should be translated as "the will to power", in which state the veil is removed from the mind.

At the end of 1920 Gibran met Tagore, an Indian poet and spiritualist, at a party in his honor. They argued about matter and spirit, Tagore vehemently criticizing the American people for their materialism and greed. Gibran retorted that Tagore was misled since spirit manifests itself even in machines. The material and the spiritual are one and not contradictory, he insisted. Spirit, Gibran asserted, exists in all life and things. This rather primitive pantheistic standpoint is not much different than that held by the naked and awed savage in the midst of the primordial forest who, unable to distinguish between mind and matter, believes himself bound up in the "oneness" of the great flux of being. It is a being without differentiation or distinction, without beginning and without end. Anything but a new and bold intellectual assertion, this atavistic aberration can be found in all that Gibran wrote and is at the root of Gibran's refusal to distinguish between religions, let alone accept one.

The heroine, Amina, of *Lofty Pillars*, characterizes this attitude. When asked about the beginnings of religion she replies, "There is no God but God and nothing but God . . ." This is typically nebulous just as are his assertions about love. What Gibran means by love is very difficult to say, however. For instance, in *The Prophet*, he tells us that the foundation of work, pain, faith, freedom of marriage, and "the link that ties the mind to the heart" is love, but he never defines just what love is. Obviously it is not the love promoted by religion, nor is it romantic love. Love is rather a vague quality that permeates the whole of human existence. The secret behind existence is love, says Gibran, a secret judgment probably derived from his fuzzy idea about the unity of existence. If we are all unified, if we are all one then we should love one another as we love ourselves. Not to do so would be to go against nature, a nature that is concretized and epitomized in the conciousness and existence of Man.

Sharing importance with Gibran's bizarre approach to the unity of existence is the idea of reincarnation which, no doubt, received in its formulation some inspiration from Nietzsche's doctrine of eternal recurrences. One of the fundamental ideas of Zarathustra is that of the eternal recurrence as the highest expression and unique formula of the "yea-saying" attitude toward life. Like Nietzsche, Gibran had abandoned the idea of heaven and hell. As a consequence, squaring nicely with his idea of the continuous stream and unified existence of the universe, is the idea of eternal recurrence or reincarnation whereby man comes back again and again to play out his part and to rise to higher and higher levels until, possibly, he achieves the level of the superman.

It is the spirit or doctrine of the eternal recurrence that sets the seal to eternity and the world of becoming. The idea of reincarnation in both Nietzsche and Gibran is a test of the strength of man, his ability to say yes to life rather than turn his back upon it. Nietzsche speaks of the world-approving man who shouts "Again" to life over and over. The reason why Gibran laid stress on the theory of recurrence was the same as that of Nietzsche: it seemed to fill a gap in his philosophy. It confers on the intangible flux of becoming the concrete embodiment of being and continuity without the interjection of a metaphysical entity that hovers over the universe. But while Nietzsche avoids the introduction of a transcendent deity, he also avoids pantheism in the subtle reintroduction of the concept of God under the name of the universe. Gibran was unable to distinguish between a false and spurious concept of the universe and traditional pantheism. The theory of reincarnation excludes the idea of immortality while at the same time providing a substitute for this idea—even if the notion of living one's life over and over again a countless number of times is likely to inspire only limited zeal. To both Nietzsche and Gibran the theory of the eternal recurrence expresses their resolute acceptance of this worldiness. While in Nietzsche this was necessary because of his atheism, it is more difficult to understand its appearance in Gibran since he never really was devoted to atheism but rather was suspended between total belief and total rejection. Therefore, his own expression of this doctrine appears illogical and the least intelligent of the two.

The universe is, for both men, shut in as it were; its significance is purely imminent. It is the strong and artistic man who, being at the same time poet and prophet, will affirm this universe and create and face life with steadfastness, courage and "joy". Nietzsche's theory of the eternal recurrence rules out the concept of superman as the final end of a non-repeatable creative process. In Gibran, as in Nietzsche, the idea of God is inextricably bound up with the concept of man as the being who confers intelligibility on the world and creates values. Because he believed in the recurrence of the life cycle, Gibran looked upon death with optimism. In *The Prophet* he writes, "For what is it to die but stand naked in the wind and to melt into the sun?" Here he talks like a romantic and a mystic who views death as real and a bridge to higher life. Man hangs between animal and God.

Gibran believed that the universe is. There was no sense in attempting to analyze it; it existed. Conceptual thought did not best communicate the nature or reality of things but rather worthwhile and true knowledge was to be found in the wellsprings of the intuitive processes of man couched in metaphor and poetic imagery. In a letter to Mary Haskell he had written, "I do not seek to dissect the universe but to seek in myself. After all, reality is indivisible and hence, unanalyzable insofar as we do analyze it and falsify it." Therefore, it was not the scientific-analytic but the intuitive-emotional approach that he preferred. Intuition wrapped in poetic metaphor epitomized the essence of Gibran's thought which attempts to take us to the very inwardness of life. The intellect is not in any sense in touch with reality. Gibran also seems to have been caught up as a recruit in a fairly wide-spread reaction against science and technology in the years immediately preceding and following World War I. The chief result of this offensive was to vindicate and to rehabilitate forms of immediate experience, such as literature, religion, and most important of all, at least in relation to Gibran, various mystical or nonrational experiences. Both Nietzsche and Henri Bergson were self-proclaimed "joyous philosophers". Gibran, despite his earlier negativism, assumed the mantle of the joyful Mustafa.

Gibran had said in 1915: "We are all that there is beyond and above this world. Nothing exists between us and eternity." And it was precisely upon this premise that *The Prophet* was written. But *The Prophet* is not a very profound work. Its language is, on a very superficial level, at times beautiful, but it is neither original nor clear, trying as it does to couch traditional *maxims* of Christianity and philosophy in an extraordinarily subjective and intellectually inconclusive poetic form. Just as without the intelligent baton of the conductor music is incoherent and meaningless since it lacks discipline, direction, and structure, so it is with *The Prophet*. Words without meaning, imperatives without thought, music without direction all come to the same thing.

The Prophet's greatest failing, however, is its lack of social responsibility and its ahistorical approach to human existence. There is a lack of perspective and realism in Gibran. He sees things in simplistic ways, offering simplistic solutions. He was, in truth, alienated from the vital currents of the culture in which he lived. He was a man who existed in his own solipsistic world, revealing to people how they should think and act and live without really ever understanding them or the real world they lived in —a world he himself was estranged from. Nowhere in *The Prophet* is there a sign that the advice he gives can be applied on a realistic level to the way people think and live. Because it lacks a true sense of social and cultural responsibility, *The Prophet* is, in many ways, an essentially regressive and immature work, reflecting the immaturity, primitivism and naiveté of Gibran. What he is saying is neither new nor is it original; philosophers, holy men, and poets have said everything he says in a more profound, equally beautiful, and infinitely more realistic manner.

But there are those who after the writing of his *Prophet* likened Gibran to a saint—a man unimpressed by the myriad temptations of flesh and spirit. Gibran was, nevertheless, not a saint, and nothing better than the following episode can remind us of this. Na'ima relates that one day Gibran received a letter from a young woman asking to see him, so impressed was she by *The Prophet*. Flattered, Gibran called the young woman and asked if she would like to come to his apartment. Elated at her good fortune, she accepted, and while he recited from *The Prophet*, she listened enthralled. Before she left she confessed that in him she had "finally found a true spiritual leader and true spiritual perfection." Greatly pleased, as he always was by any praise, he encouraged her to return and the visits continued. Finally Gibran seduced her and, her faith shattered, she never returned again. She wrote him telling that when she had first met him she thought he was "true superman" and an example to all men. But much to her disappointment, she lamented, he was no different from other men with actions totally divorced from words. Dismayed by this letter the sensitive Gibran wrote and implored her to forgive him and to restore her faith in life. She should not, he told her, judge God by the man Gibran's actions. Obviously feeling very guilty, he even asked her to marry him.

The abstract imagery, the nebulous language, the uncertain emotion of *The Prophet*, all of these are antithetical to the more concise, more realistic and more demanding Western mind. While his early works showed a certain relevancy to the social and economic problems of an Eastern society out of step with the twentieth century, the works of Gibran have little, if any, relevance to the Western ethos. Gibran could not challenge the Western literary world and assert himself in it with the equipment he had, but could only appeal on a popular level to puerile emotionalism and seekers after the exotic. He was, as mentioned earlier, an anachronism, a man with a style, a vision, and a message that was out of step with the time. Men were looking to Eliot, Pound, and Yeats, to the contemporary streams of symbolism, naturalism, realism. A primitive theology, a basic alienation from the real world, and an anachronistic style were to condemn Gibran to the limbo of mediocrity with a popularity and recognition of a conventional rather than a critical kind.

Gibran had finished the first draft of *The Prophet* in 1921. As early as 1920, while he was in the midst of writing it, he had written to Mary Haskell stating that "This work shall incorporate all that I am. It is the crowning summit of my being, of my life, of my work. In *The Prophet* I have set forth certain principles that I should like to be the living proof of the righteousness of my position. Merely writing these principles would mean to have false principles, I can only accept these principles by living them." Gibran's resolve personifies a Nietzschean admonition. Nietzsche had urged time and time again that those who believe in philosophy must live it, that is, they must be the living incarnation of their convictions.

Many believe that the Nietzschean phase of Gibran's intellectual formation had been gotten over prior to the creation of *The Prophet*, despite the fact that *The Prophet* had reflected much of Nietzsche. What is more, Gibran was not to leave Nietzsche behind after completing *The Prophet*. In 1928, in a strange book titled *Jesus, the Son of Man*, he wrote, through the vehicle of James, the son of Zebedee:

> . . . numerous are the worms that slither around my feet but no matter how hard I try I shall never be able to destroy them completely. My soul is weary of feeling sympathy for these slithering beings who consider me a coward because I did not wish to walk amongst their city walls and aid in the fortification of their human fortresses. It is a shame that I should have need to indulge in mercy for these beings to the very end. How I wish that I could direct myself to a world, a world greater than this one, one where there would be men because they are great, deserving my solicitude and my presence.

Thus we have a Messiah, a Jesus figure whom Gibran pictured as much better than, but extremely intolerant and disdainful of, those whom he had come to have mercy upon and save. The figure of Zarathustra and, therefore, the influence of Nietzsche, is apparent in Gibran's characterization of this Jesus. No longer was he merely someone with a message of pure love and passive acceptance, but a man who, harboring a powerful will, was neither weak nor poor, nor a worker of miracles. He was a strong man, first and foremost. In short, he was Gibran, artist and poet who, having a deeper insight into the mysteries of existence, would lead men out of their miserable state of being.

There is a contradiction involved here, however. Gibran has Jesus denouncing men as not worthy of his mercy or his teaching, but, at the same time, Gibran's prophet—Jesus—has come among mankind in order to save them from themselves. This probably mirrors how Gibran himself felt. Alone, neglected, this self-styled twentieth century prophet probably felt a degree of rancor against the benign unconcern and cavalier neglect that he received from the intellectual and literary world at large. A man alienated from those around him, he found it easy to curse people for being ungrateful and unworthy of his teaching while at the same time they were everywhere in need of his uplifting message. Gibran's works are filled with inconsistencies of this type. On the one side he gives in to what are probably personal feelings and on the other he forgets them, and wrapping himself in a Messiah complex, finds himself once more compelled to spiritually inspire the masses and save the world.

Gibran treaded two parallel but distinct pathways: that of his persecuted self and that of the prophet, who would, from his lofty position, solace, save and sanctify the people. Which one was really Gibran? Was the cloak of the prophet just that—a cover for his true feelings of alienation, guilt and hatred, or was he really the loving prophet who was, unfortunately, unable to maintain *ad continuum* the lofty attitude that such a position demanded? Gibran was, after all, a man tortured by self-doubts, including guilt about his yearning for fame and wealth—feelings, however, which did not always last for long. Even though he was more than willing to observe and criticize and help do away with the faults of others, he never really saw his own.

Gibran was obsessed by the idea of being a prophet. Once he told Mary Haskell in a letter that one night he had a wonderful dream: filled as it was with images of the tallness of his body. But when he woke up in the morning and cast aside the covers to see his small and frail frame, reality impinged once more upon fantasy and he became extremely disconsolate. This dream might be a clue into his assumption of the prophet's role, a prophet whose physical appearance was as imposing as his soaring spirit.

In September of 1910, finding himself in difficult financial straits, Gibran reluctantly returned to Boston and Huwayyik went back to Lebanon. In 1912 Gibran moved from Boston to New York where he rented a studio at 51 West 10th Street between Fifth and Sixth Avenues. This was his home until his death in 1931.

Huwayyik continued to live out the rest of his life between Europe and Lebanon. He produced many pieces of art, mainly sculpture, and they still survive in Lebanon. In the 1950's he announced his intention to write his memoirs about Gibran in Paris with the aid of Edvic Juraydini Shaybub. They were finally published in 1957, nine years before Huwayyik's death in 1966.

Many years before, in 1899, Gibran and Huwayyik stood on a mountain top under some cedar trees above the pleasant and sleepy village of Bsharri which lay before them in the valley. Bsharri was covered with a dense fog while they, some distance above it, could see the clear, blue sky. Turning to Huwayyik, Gibran commented, "People in Bsharri see nothing but fog, but we see clear sky behind it because we stand on the peak of Western influence, and because of this we are born to reform the world." A noble but somewhat unrealistic assertion.

CHAPTER ONE

MADEMOISELLE OLGA

☐ In the spring of 1909, when I had only been a short time in Paris and was still trying to organize my affairs and my studies, I met every now and then with Gibran—who had preceded me to that city—asking him about various matters in order to benefit from his experience and direction. One day, while we were eating lunch in a small restaurant near the Luxembourg Gardens, I noticed that Gibran was distracted and not giving me his full attention. When I asked him where his thoughts were, he replied, "Why be preoccupied with life's problems now, Yusuf? Turn to your left and look at that beautiful girl over there, eating slowly and reading a book. I have been watching her and noticing that she is stealing glances at you. Haven't you felt those honey-colored eyes of hers upon you?"

I turned in the direction Gibran indicated and saw those eyes he had described staring at me—only to be immediatley lowered to her plate and book. I looked at her carefully. She was bare-headed and had blonde hair. Her face had a bright purity about it, her hands were very white, and around her shoulders she wore a grey shawl trimmed with brocade. After some thought I told Gibran, "This girl is no Parisian. I wonder where she is from?"

For the second time the girl raised her head and looked in our direction and, noticing that we were looking at her, immediately bowed her head to her book. "It seems to me that she is not an ordinary girl," Gibran observed.

49

"She has a noble appearance. Maybe she is a Scandinavian student."

After this conjecture, we once again resumed the discussion of our own affairs. It seemed that Gibran was not content with having joined the Julien Académie. The noisy atmosphere did not suit his temperament, and he didn't feel he was learning anything from his teacher at that school, Jean Paul Laurence. As a matter of fact, he believed that Laurence was the last person in the world he could learn anything from. Besides, his name was not known in America at all—a point that was somehow important to Gibran. "Yusuf," he firmly told me, "I am seriously thinking of working in my own studio, free and independent. What do you say to sharing the fees for a model?"

I replied, "This suits me fine, for I have no wish to become attached to a specific academy. We could work in the morning at your studio because the light is better there than in mine, and in the afternoon and evening we could go to the free art academies. And, if we should find a model whom we like, we can pay the fee ourselves and work in the way we want to."

"Excellent, excellent," Gibran answered. "That's a good idea. We should also visit the museums of Paris and the public and private exhibitions in order to become more closely acquainted with what is going on in the art world. It seems to me that Paris is experiencing a kind of revolution in painting. What lunacy! Art is not a plaything! Art, like writing, is a medium for the expression of feeling. I intend to write about this idea soon."

I looked toward our blonde friend and saw that she was paying the waitress for her lunch and was about to leave. Clasping her grey shawl and her book to her breast, her slender body swayed gracefully as she walked in our direction. As she passed in front of our table she graciously nodded without smiling or saying anything. We approved of this amenity, and Gibran remarked, "Now that we have become acquainted without saying a word, we really should find out whether the greeting was for you or for me."

"Either way we won't duel over it," I answered.

In connection with this tenuous acquaintanceship, Gibran likened our situation to the way celestial bodies in the vast firmament draw close to one another and then move apart. I prodded him jokingly, "And if there is a collision?"

Gibran slowly smiled and said, "That would be an interesting subject for a story which I have often thought of writing. At present I am searching for heroes; and for the present, at least, I like Balzac's heroes."

The waitress came, carrying a dish of fruit, and Gibran said, "Tell us, Georgette, what do you know about the girl in the grey shawl?"

"She is Mademoiselle Olga," Georgette replied. "I think she is a Russian. She studies at the Sorbonne. She always has a book in her hand. Poor thing, she does not seem to have any friends."

After Georgette had left, Gibran resumed his discussion of Balzac, telling how Balzac used to wander through the streets of Paris at night wearing Oriental dress and gathering impressions. He would then return before dawn to his room, draw the damask drapes, drink coffee, and plunge into his writing. "It was thus that Rodin portrayed him," he said, "but the statue that he made was not widely appreciated until half a century later when it was placed on a pedestal where the boulevards Raspail and Montparnasse meet. There, it has since become one of the most charming sights in Paris."

On the next day we returned to the same restaurant and sat in the same place, discussing, while we ate, literature and art as well as our own affairs. While so engaged, Mademoiselle Olga came in, slender and graceful, once again holding her grey shawl and a book to her breast, anxiously searching for an empty table. At that time in the Latin Quarter it was the custom, when the restaurants were crowded, for people to share a table and not consider it an inconvenience.

"Invite her, Yusuf," Gibran urged.

"Invite her yourself, Gibran!"

While we were hesitating, Mademoiselle Olga showed

more courage than either of us and, slowly walking up to our table, inquired very politely, "Gentlemen, would you allow me to join you? I will not be a bother to you."

Instantly we made room for her. Gibran began to speak to her in English, which she spoke fluently. Noting that I had not entered into the conversation, she soon turned to me and asked, in French, if I too spoke English. I answered that I did not.

"It is more appropriate, then," she said, "that all of us speak in French, the language of this country." She asked what our native language was and we answered that it was Arabic. She replied, "How nice it would be if I could study it! The study of Oriental languages falls within the scope of my field of specialization."

The waitress returned, carrying a plate of hors d'oeuvres, and asked Mademoiselle Olga if she cared to order. Mademoiselle Olga looked at our plates, pointed toward them, and said, "Bring me some risotto, rabbit stew, and Russian salad."

She began to explain to the waitress how to prepare the Russian salad, but Georgette assured her that she knew how to do this. Before she left, however, the waitress whispered to her, "Take care of yourself, and don't let these two scare you. You are not so inexperienced that you should not know that two are less dangerous than one. Experience has thus taught the girls of Paris. Have confidence!"

While we slowly ate, we became better acquainted.

"I am Olga G., and I come from the city of Tomsk in Siberia. It is a journey of fifteen days by train from Paris."

She had come to Paris she explained, to continue her education in rhetoric, French literature, and music, so that eventually she would be able to oversee these disciplines at the University of Tomsk, of which her father was the president.

"And I am Gibran from Lebanon," Gibran answered in English, "who had immigrated with his mother, his sisters, and his brother to the United States, and whom Providence has aided to come to Paris to learn more about art and to work at writing. I find great pleasure in writing and drawing and have many things to tell the world."

Olga turned towards me with a questioning look in her eyes. I said, "I, too, was born in a small and obscure village in the mountains of Lebanon. I have come to Paris via Rome to work, as befits my inclinations, at painting and sculpture, astronomy, and the art of life."

At this point, Olga interrupted me and in a serious tone said, "This is vague, monsieur. It is necessary for a man to have a clear goal in life toward which he should actively strive. Show me your palm!"

I remained mute to her observation but willingly stretched out my palm. She began to study the lines of my palm carefully, without saying a word. Then she turned to Gibran's palm, doing the same thing. I decided to show that, like her, I knew something of palm reading and astrology, so I took her delicate hand in mine and examined the veins on the back of it and the lines on the palm. For some time I had noticed how the lines in people's palms differ and had concluded that they usually do have a relationship to behavior and character. How great was my astonishment when I found, for the first time, a palm which had the same pattern of lines as my own!

While we were sipping our coffee and Gibran was smoking a cigarette—and how he loved coffee and cigarettes—Gibran began to speak of different types of women. Because he had very bad impressions of Eastern women, he judged them harshly, and in this context he mentioned the tragic heroine of one of his stories, Warda al-Hani, who had deserted her husband. He used this subject to launch into an attack upon human attitudes. "Most people, Yusuf," he deplored, "wallow in a sea of lying, treachery, and meanness. They claim to be the enemies of outmoded laws and traditions. I, in turn, am the enemy of this hypocrisy and duplicity and I shall tell them this in order to shame them."

"And if they did not read what you had written and did not become ashamed, wouldn't your labor then have been in vain since people will remain as they have always

53

been?" I asked. I then quoted a passage from Voltaire: "Most people will always remain liars and hypocrites, cunning and ungrateful thieves, weaklings, idiots, reckless charlatans, avaricious drunkards, misers, bloodshedders, dishonorable fanatics, and cowards."

After this conversation we left the restaurant and took a walk in the beautiful park close to the restaurant. We stopped for a while at a pond where children were sailing their cardboard boats. Gibran mused out loud, "I wish I were one of them. Do you remember, Yusuf, the kites we used to fly in the sky of Beirut and on the Ashrafiyya Heights? I once tried to fly a kite in the sky of Boston but I was stopped by the police."

We walked on and Gibran said, pointing out a row of statues, "And these are the statues of the Queens of France; each one is wearing a different costume, as if they were fashion models."

"Do you agree with me," I asked, "that this queen looks like Mademoiselle Olga?"

"You mean," he answered, "Mademoiselle Olga looks like the statue of this queen!"

CHAPTER TWO

THE ART BOOKSHOP

☐ When we got to the rue d'Assas I noticed an active beehive on the curb. I stopped Gibran and for a while we watched the activity of the bees bringing raw materials to the hive for conversion into wax and honey, while the drones, impeding their work, loitered stupidly around its entrance. Gibran joked, "See how dull these drones are? The bees shouldn't be blamed if they deserted them."

"That would be a delightful subject for a story, Gibran," I volunteered. "Why don't you try it? And don't forget to explain that if insects follow *their* instincts, how much more man follows his instincts . . ."

Gibran answered laughing, "That's also one of Voltaire's ideas. I notice that you frequently quote his opinions. Is there any relationship between you two?"

"A remote relationship, anyway," I answered. "I like his charming personality, the humor in his writings, and that sharp tongue from whose lashes no one was safe. What is more important is that he shook up his contemporaries. He awakened them to their miserable status, and pointed to the source of their malady. How pale and barren are those Oriental writers who were the contemporaries of Voltaire, and even those who came after him. They engaged in nothing but futile chattering, empty praise, versification and erotic love 'poetry'."

Gibran was slow to respond. He was drowned in contemplation absorbing what I had said. Finally he said, "The East is a barren wasteland and the atmosphere is dull, lifeless, and decadent. I am determined, Yusuf, to shake the nerves of the Americans and to sound my trumpet in *their* midst. Their country is prosperous and their dollars are endless. They are a wealthy people and, like all rich people, blind and selfish. May God curse money! How it stands between man and his aspirations!"

Gibran often ended our conversations with this last statement while complaining of his own circumstances and the barriers to his own unfulfilled aspirations. He wanted to soar high, to release and to reveal these ideas which contended in his heart and mind; but for the time being there was nothing in his wings except delicate down which was unable to carry his giant being to the heights he sought.

We turned and walked over to the rue Vavin, between the Luxembourg Gardens and Montparnasse, where there were some free art institutes for painting and sculpture. At that time, in the midst of these institutes stood a small art book shop whose window was always decorated with a charming variety of books, magazines, and cubistic paintings. Gibran and I stopped in front of this book shop examining the display with no intention of entering, especially since the books seemed to be expensive.

While we were looking at the display, we saw a brunette looking at us from behind the window, greeting us with a cheerful smile and black eyes—eyes which Gibran thought were flirtatious. She opened the door, saying, "Come in, gentlemen. There are many books and magazines inside. You can browse and read without buying anything. However, we do have a ten percent discount."

We entered, of course, and with the brunette was another girl. She was blonde, younger than the first girl, and had a charming air about her. Her hair fell to her shoulders in a delightfully feminine way. She walked toward us, asking candidly, "Are you Spanish or Italian?"

With the same candor, Gibran answered, pointing his hand as if towards a far away place, saying, "We are from there, from Lebanon. Me, from Jerusalem, and from Heaven."

When they heard Gibran's answer, the two girls shouted, and the younger one, beaming with joy, said,

56

"Ah Jerusalem! We are Jews from Romania. Our grandfather is in Jerusalem. He went there several years ago to be buried in the Holy Land so that after his death he might ascend to Heaven and the bosom of our father, Abraham."

Her laughter was laced with a slight note of mockery which I appreciated. Sharing her laughter, I said to her, "I hope your grandfather will live to a very old age—older even than Methuselah!"

Soon we were all acquainted. The older one, Suzanne, was "older than twenty-five", not the age of Methuselah, but *our* age, and the younger one, Leah, was about fifteen.

When Suzanne discovered that we were involved with painting she asked, "Which kind?" When we answered that we were still engrossed in the traditional approach to painting, she immediately replied, "No demand for it," and began pointing to the drawings and paintings around the shop. Some of them were cubistic, and there were others whose style I did not recognize, in which female figures appeared crooked and distorted, as if seen through concave or convex mirrors.

I pointed to one painting which was especially distorted and jokingly asked Leah, for by this time I had noticed that she had a sense of humor, "Is this a painting of you, Mademoiselle? And are these the shapes of your body under your dress?"

We all laughed except Gibran, whose face had turned red with the blood of anger. He entered into the conversation, but with a very different tone. Pointing his cane at the paintings, he said, "Have these lunatics forgotten their mothers and sisters and sweethearts? Or have they lost every feeling and ignored every standard in order to distort the body of woman in this manner—the divine and holy body of woman."

He was speaking with such feeling that Leah was baffled and didn't know what to say. Suzanne interrupted him, trying to quell his anger, and explained the economic aspects of the question to him. "There is a demand for this kind of art," she informed him.

Gibran, however, was not satisfied with this explanation, and continued his sermon, saying, "From the Stone Age to the present, the artist has sung the praises of the body and the beauty of woman, indeed of any beauty. Is this kind of art the last song which the artist will sing in honor of woman? Art is not made for business, Mademoiselle!"

At this moment a tall and handsome young man came in. Suzanne introduced him as the owner of the book shop and her relative. The man stretched his hand out to greet us and introduced himself: "Calmie."

"Gibran."

The younger girl, Leah, mimicked Gibran's hand movement and said, "From there—from Jerusalem."

We lost no time, and immediately entered into a discussion about art and painting. When Calmie learned that we preferred classical art, he repeated Suzanne's words, "No demand for it." Gibran turned away from us, carefully examining some books in silence.

Calmie took me aside, asking whether it was possible to see some of my work. I told him that my studio was only a walk of about five minutes from the shop, and that we had plenty of time, because the art institute did not open until three. Gibran said in Arabic, "Accompany him alone, Yusuf. I will wait here, reading and browsing until you return."

Calmie and I went by the road which divides the Montparnasse Cemetery into two parts. We walked past the imposing tombs, and stopped for a moment in front of the tomb of Baudelaire, contemplating the statue of him which, unfortunately, had fallen on its back. The color of the marble had become pale and worn from the rain and the sun. Calmie recited: "When you rest, O my stern beautiful one, in the depth of a black marble tomb . . ." and then continued walking without finishing the poem, saying, "this is not the time for poetry."

We turned left on to the rue Freideveaux and I opened the door to my studio, which overlooked the street. Calmie preceded me, saying, "This looks more like a sculptor's studio than a painter's studio."

He wandered around, pausing in front of each painting, most of which were unfinished. Among the paintings was one of a seated woman with seven spears piercing her chest. I noticed that he looked at it with a mixture of disapproval and scorn, and I felt sweat on my forehead.

He asked, "What does this portrait represent?"

Pretending to be calm, I answered, "It is a portrait of the Virgin Mary, the Mother of Seven Sorrows. Sister Therese, one of the Sisters of Charity, asked me to paint it. I have sisters who are nuns." Calmie stared at me in a manner which annoyed me. Then he pointed to a picture of a man who was kneeling in an attitude of prayerful humility. Again the scornful look appeared on Calmie's face and he inquired, "And this one?"

"It is of Christ in the Garden of Olives."

"Did the Sisters of Charity request this one also?" he asked. "This, my friend, is rather far removed from the fashion. If your artistic objective is to save your soul and if you are concerned with showing sympathy to the nuns, then that is a private matter which concerns you alone and with which I have nothing to do. However, if you want to make money, this is not the way. Believe me, there is no market for this kind of art. Listen to me. Try cubism, and if you succeed with it, I will guarantee the selling of your paintings. It's a simple matter of arithmetic: one plus one equals two! Ten percent of the price for me!"

Later, I told Gibran about this conversation and said that I had taken Calmie's words seriously and that I intended to try to paint in the cubistic manner. Gibran chastised me, "How many times have I told you that art is not a game or a business? It is a means to express feeling. It is a divine breath. It is . . . I can't find a word to express what I want to say."

After this unfinished outburst of thought and feeling, Gibran calmed down and continued, saying, "In my opinion, you should work with sculpture. There are no sculptors in the Arab East and you will be the first. And if you wish to go with me to the United States, the opportunity there is even greater."

Neither Gibran nor I was really aware at that time of the tragic condition of the arts in the East.

CHAPTER THREE

LE DÔME CAFÉ

☐ Anyone who wishes to discuss the social life of the Latin Quarter at that time, that is, shortly before the First World War, must mention the Dôme Café, which was located at the corner where the boulevards Raspail and Montparnasse meet. The Dôme enjoyed a wide popularity, and the inhabitants of the Latin Quarter preferred it to all other cafés because of its unique character. It was the meeting place for writers, artists, and assorted intellectuals of every type. Around its oblong tables sat a strange mixture of people, incessantly discussing and arguing over almost every conceivable subject, including art, literature and world events. To make the atmosphere more complete, every now and then a Moroccan wearing a big red tassled fez paraded before the clients with his wares of carpets, tablecloths, sashes, neckties, and other assorted goods dangling from his shoulders. In his pockets he carried contraband, to which he made reference with secret gestures. Regardless of whether he sold anything or not, he would constantly parade before the tables and seemed to us as if he were from a strange world, a world existing on the margins of civilization.

Sitting in the Dôme was an art in itself. Not everyone could perfect this art and, consequently, enjoy its advantages. Blessed be God who created people of different tastes! For example, Gibran refused to sit in this café, and often told me, "It is a waste of time, Yusuf." He preferred the American custom of discussing things "face to face" quietly. He liked to walk along the banks of the Seine or stroll through the old streets of Paris like his "friend" Balzac. He did not stay too late at night clubs or cafés. He had a delicate constitution and preferred to go to bed early, or to spend his time thinking and writing.

Mademoiselle Olga was like him in this respect. Only once could I persuade her to come with me to the Dôme to see what it was like. Once there she felt uncomfortable in the crowded and noisy atmosphere, heavy with smoke, and she would not try it again. She, too, did not like to sit in a crowd.

Our "group", consisting of Suzanne, Leah, Calmie, Dr. Casper, the sculptor Christesco, myself, and others, had mastered the art of sitting in the Dôme, and we often practiced our skill. When one of us came early, he made a payment and reserved a table so that when the rest came they were sure of a place to sit. After spending the afternoon working in the Art Academy, I anxiously looked forward to these enjoyable evenings.

The Academy was operated by Catherine, an Italian woman who had worked as a model in her youth. When she retired, after training several models, she was entrusted with the administration of the Academy.

I remember how extensive Madame Catherine's knowledge was in all fields relating to her profession. Furthermore, no secret would escape her. Time had given her an intuitive knowledge of human nature and by simply looking into the eyes of the students she could anticipate their thoughts, troubles and aspirations.

The first time I heard her speak French I noted her peculiar accent, and I never doubted for a moment that she was an Italian. I made a point of speaking to her in that language and this removed any barrier that might have existed between us.

The Academy contained four studios for painting. In one of them the model sat for three quarters of an hour and then rested for the other quarter. In the second studio the model would change his position every quarter of an hour. Sometimes I paid the fee for the lesson and sometimes I did not, and I worked whenever I liked without any objection. When Madame Catherine came to trust me, she authorized me to choose the positions of the models and to observe and supervise the students in the studio, provided that I did this politely and did not annoy my colleagues. At times I overstepped my authority and aided some of the younger female students by assigning them a more favorable position in relation to distance and light, while defying the angry looks from the young male students. These latter, Gibran and I had agreed, were a dull lot.

The Academy was open for three periods between nine in the morning and nine in the evening. Gibran preferred to attend during the last period, but even then he did not often attend.

It was my habit, as I have mentioned, to visit the Dôme Café after I was through with my lessons. I would find my friends waiting for me and I would distribute the paintings I had with me. Then it would not be long before I became deeply immersed with them in a whirlpool of scientific, artistic, political, and business discussions which went on and on almost without end: how sugar could be extracted from coal; how Coquelin and Van Gogh were able to change the course of art; how Blériot flew over the English Channel; how England was no longer an island; how the German people were industrious but the Emperor Wilhelm was frightful; how the French look upon their defeats as if they were victories . . .

When I tired of these discussions I would turn toward Leah, stroking her beautiful hair and asking her, "To whom does this hair belong?"

She would answer, "To Leah."

I would then correct her by telling her, "Just say 'Leah' and then you will be speaking Arabic!"

Sometimes, the two of us would exchange anecdotes and witty stories about the Jews, and oftimes I would whisper in her ear, "And if Abraham were insincere in his promises?"

Laughing, she would answer, "If Abraham were insincere then nothing would make any sense." But then she would continue, "It is more likely that he was not sincere. What do you think?"

She used to lead me with innocent cunning into telling stories about priests, saying, "My friend, pray tell just another small story." And when I would hesitate, she would urge me on by saying, "Once upon a time there was a respected priest . . ."

As I had learned the skills of Scheherazade to some degree of perfection and had also learned to improvise, I would nimbly complete the story. Then we would laugh and chuckle together until we made so much noise that the rest of our companions would envy us.

So this is how things went with Leah. As for her older sister, Suzanne, whenever she found the opportunity to talk to me privately she whispered her ideas about the nature and philosophy of love into my ears. How often she would say: "I can't understand why people place so much importance on love. They make it a god. They build temples to it. They compose their tenderest poetry about it. They fight and even commit suicide over it. It has even been concluded that love is an ounce of honey over a ton of wood. What strange reasoning this is! In reality love is the simplest of all things—it is like a drink of water. Don't you agree with me?"

When I ignored her conversations about love, she would change the subject, making a new proposal: a trip with her to China!

"We will be one month going," she said, "and one month coming back, and one month in Peking and in other cities where we can negotiate with the concerns which specialize in handicrafts. There is a demand in Paris for these goods. Then we could open a store right here in Paris. And then if destiny unites Leah and Gibran in marriage, we will then leave the store in their charge and travel, both of us, all over the wide world. I like to travel, just as you do, isn't it so? We can visit India and Japan, conducting business transactions there. Before long our shop will become one of the biggest businesses in Paris and money will pile up in our hands! Believe me, my friend, art and literature will not provide bread for man."

In this way, Suzanne used to go on, discussing her

money-making schemes with me and attempting to entice me to share in them. Once Calmie found out about part of her business plans and shaking his head in ridicule he told her, "Don't tire yourself, Suzanne. The last thing that our friend Yusuf would think of is business. Don't you see that he gets confused even when buying a pair of socks? He would probably lose five francs in the deal. It seems to me that he runs away from money as if there were an enmity between the two of them. Instead of concentrating on artistic works which would bring him plenty of money—and this would be possible if he listened to me—he wastes his time in futile and useless studies, like the history of mankind, the development of civilization, astronomy and the philosophy of religion. Are there any subjects of less material value in the world?"

Whenever Gibran and I discussed this subject, he would get upset and say, while thrusting his finger at my face, "To China, and with a young Jewish brunette with a flirtatious manner? To whom love is like a drink of water? This is sheer madness, Yusuf. I absolutely forbid you even to joke about this subject." I would retort, joking, "And if destiny arranges for you to marry Leah!"

Interrupting me with his nervous, sardonic laugh, shaking his head, he would grumble, "That is just what I need—Leah!"

At other times he would continue in a serious tone, "This is no time for joking, Yusuf, I am surprised at how you waste your time this way. We should strive to understand the currents of artistic activity in Paris and this mad revolt which is in full swing against art and beauty, this violent battle between the imitation of nature and a turning against it. This morning I saw some paintings which really perplexed me. I asked myself whether it would be more appropriate to copy or imitate nature according to the methods of these contemporary lunatics. What if we neglect structure, perspective, and meticulous observation? What if we sacrificed that most prominent aspect of beauty which is line and form as they appear to the sound eye, divesting art of its most significant elements?

65

These are the questions for which we should find answers, not the questions of Suzanne, Leah, and a journey to China!"

After this sermon, I presently found myself elevated into Gibran's world, united with him in deep and serious thinking. We began to discuss and analyze the reasons for the artistic revolution which had begun to sweep Paris, a revolution which was dividing artists into different camps while leaving a large question mark in the minds of the more conservative among them.

CHAPTER FOUR

WITH GIBRAN
AT THE LOUVRE

☐ Every Sunday, admission to the Louvre was free. Therefore, it was natural that beginning artists and art students, especially impecunious ones, waited for Sundays so that they could visit the richest museum in the world. Gibran and I divided the rest of the week with typical Bohemian haphazardness between work and private endeavors. If we differed over something, each of us went his own way, but we never differed over meeting at the Louvre every Sunday.

We eagerly anticipated our weekly visits to that museum and went there like worshipful pilgrims visiting a holy shrine. We spent happy hours in the various galleries filled with immortal masterpieces of art, which ran the gamut from ancient times to the twentieth century.

One day, while visiting the Louvre in our usual state of excitement, enthralled by the masterpieces around us, each of us agreed that he could remain there forever.

I turned to Gibran and said with tears in my eyes, "Should we throw all of this magnificent legacy into the trash bin just because some charlatans, unable to achieve mastery in art, switched paths, hoping to discover something new? Their strange and distorted forms would make even bereaved mothers laugh."

Gibran was pleased to hear me so positively launch into one of our favorite subjects. We had frequently talked about this problem, but had never really penetratingly analyzed it. He laughed so loudly that everyone in the hall heard him as he said, "Your pulse is strong today, Yusuf. I admire your spirit but unfortunately your premise is weak. Don't you think there could be something behind this new movement? If we exerted an effort to really understand it then we could say that our freedom to follow our own inclinations would be greater. A type of art—whether it be a painting or statue or any other—which the senses and mind can easily comprehend is often commonplace, and dull, even sleep inducing! On the contrary, art which is not so easily understood—after much effort—produces great joy.

"Don't you agree with me, Yusuf, that this new type of art is an attempt at something deep? It is a type of creativity in which there is deep thought and unsurpassed pleasure."

Gibran had said what he wanted to say—revealing a modification of his own previous position—and now it was my turn to present my point of view. I said, "This is beautiful talk, to be published in periodicals and art journals and expressed by word of mouth among art critics. However, I feel that beauty has an eternal quality and that the artist who is not concerned with beauty or perfection, and who only likes distorted or garbled forms, who shuns the natural grace of line, this artist—allow me to speak frankly, Gibran—does not merit my admiration, and I predict that these galleries will never harbor his productions.

"Furthermore, do not works of art reflect the artist's impressions of his surroundings? I am familiar with every aspect of Paris which can boast of genuine beauty and I don't see any trace of these conspicuous 'disfigurations' which modern artists emulate in each other without shame. Am I blind or what?"

"These impressions are reflective of what's in their minds, Yusuf," Gibran interrupted, pointing his finger at me. "This is an interesting subject which requires deep study. I shall ponder upon it tonight."

I resumed my side of the argument with continued fervor, "Look, please look, through this window at that vast sky and the Tuilleries and the watercourse of the

Seine; see how the soft dust-diffused light lifts off the face of Paris like a transparent veil. I have often noted that every big city has its own atmosphere, a magic characteristic, or a touch of beauty, like the faces of young girls, each one of which has its own quality of charm and innocence."

Gibran listened attentively, his misty eyes staring at something far away. When I had finished he remarked, "Talking about big cities, how I desire to see Athens and to sit among the ruins of the Acropolis! I always feel a certain loss because I don't pray daily in the temple of Minerva, or because my feet don't come in contact with the earth of Rome, Florence, or Venice. I am constantly disturbed by this. How lucky you are, Yusuf, to have visited and lived in those cities! Do you think if we economized enough we would be able to save for a trip? You understand the language, so we would be spared the fees for a guide!"

Both of us laughed and I said, "A trip to those cities will cost us a lot of money! Isn't Suzanne right? Make money even if you have to go to China!"

Gibran shook his head and repeated his "proverb": "Cursed money! What a barrier it is between man and his aspirations!"

We left the Louvre and walked along the bank of the Seine, looking at books and paintings, and continuing our conversation. The gloomy evening light diffused its magical luminosity over Paris. Gibran seemed as gloomy as the evening. He turned to me and said, "At the age of twenty-five, Benjamin Franklin determined to conquer the peak of knowledge and wisdom. He accomplished what he wanted.

"Here we are at the age of twenty-seven, with great ambitions, but what have we realized of them? Tell me, Yusuf, do you notice any shortcomings in me which could be corrected?"

"I would like to ask you the same question, Gibran," I answered.

This was the state of our mental attitude at that time. I remember it very well, as if it had happened yesterday.

CHAPTER FIVE

OLGA'S STORY

☐ The Luxembourg Palace in Paris is the headquarters of the French Senate. In the section of its rich gardens which borders on the rue d'Assas there were seedling pear trees whose branches were trimmed and tied into beautiful geometric shapes. In the spring these branches looked like strings of shining beads, but surpassed them in beauty and elegance. Bees hovered over them in sweet and monotonous buzzing. When the flowers had developed into fruits, the gardener, inspired by the visitors, would individually wrap them in order to protect them from insects. And when the fruits ripened, the gardener would carry them as a magnificent present to the President of the Senate.

Close to the pear seedlings stretched an expanse of white poplar and cinchona trees. Under them stretched green expanses of lawn, sprinkled here and there with flower beds. In an isolated corner, among certain very tall and overlapping trees, Mademoiselle Olga liked to stretch on the grass reading or writing. Sometimes I shared this quiet and delightful setting with her. There, we would often have intellectual discussions.

One time when we were in the garden, Olga surprised me with a question: "Isn't this affair between both of us strange? You come from the western part of Asia, east of the Mediterranean, and I come from its eastern part, and here, in this very beautiful garden, we meet in Paris, the most fascinating of cities."

She spoke quietly, her eyes turning from me toward the house sparrows she was feeding. She would hold out

71

a crumb of biscuit as far as her arm could extend. The sparrows would draw near, first with caution and then with confidence. When they realized there was no danger, they perched on her shoulders, arms and lap and went on pecking the crumbs from between her fingers, all the time, fighting and pushing each other. I remained immobile in my place lest I move and frighten these tiny creatures which afforded us so much enjoyment. Furthermore, I did not want to disturb the intimate thoughts of Olga.

Olga said, "I am the only child of my parents. My father is a friend of Count Leo Tolstoy and the Countess is a distant relative of my mother. I remember that when I was a child my parents took me with them to visit Yasnaya Poliana. Count Leo played with me, put me on his knee, and let me fondle his beard while he discussed different subjects with my father. I remember that one day they almost quarreled because of their disagreement over the concepts of the German philosopher Nietzsche. My father admired him. Years later I read Nietzsche, but not with the enthusiasm I had expected, influenced as I was by my father's opinion."

She turned to me, asking whether I have read anything by Nietzsche. I replied, "No."

The noise of the sparrows became louder as they fought bitterly over a piece of biscuit. Pointing her finger at them, Olga gently chided them, saying, "No need to quarrel, here is a new batch of biscuits. Eat and do not fight." Then she resumed her revelations.

"Through Count Leo's efforts, the Tsar appointed my father as a member of the first Duma. He became the first president of the first Duma. Because of that, I almost entered the court of the empress Alexandra Vidrovna. But my father did not like this drift of affairs and preferred to abandon politics and the Palace in order to administer the distant Tomsk University. I remember that he once told me: 'The Palace atmosphere, my daughter, is rotten. A certain monk is doing what pleases him there, which includes corrupting the morals of good women. Count Tolstoy says that the end of the world is near.'

After a period of silence and watching the sparrows play and frolic she continued, "Poor Count Leo. He is now in a state of war with his wife. She wrote to my mother complaining about her circumstances. My mother asked me to stop in Moscow on my way to Paris and go to visit Yasnaya Poliana and kindly advise the Countess to let her husband, who is over seventy, to live his life the way he wants to without nagging him.

"I met with the Countess and it seemed that she wanted her husband to appear dignified and behave in a manner befitting the greatest writer in Russia. I have seen him with my own eyes wearing a moudjik and walking barefooted not only in the house but outside as well. He washed his shirts by hand though there were many servants to do the washing. He refused to meet visitors who came to see him from distant places; as a matter of fact, he refused adamantly and for no reason to see visitors at all. He associated with the peasants and gave them most of his property and possessions. Once he told me, 'The shoes of the peasant, Olga, in my opinion, are equal to wealth and honor. I know nobles. I was one of them. I will never forget as long as I live, how one morning, after spending the night in a palace filled with food, wine, entertainment and dancing, I found, toward dawn, the poor coachman frozen to death in his seat waiting for me. O, daughter! how could I forget that sight? I assure you that the way things are will not last long. The end of the world is near.'"

Olga continued, "While the Count was thus confiding in me, speaking in a humane and compassionate way, I seized the opportunity and whispered the name of the Countess in an attempt to reconcile them. But no sooner did I do this than the Count became furious, stared at me and adamantly said, 'In their married life, a man and a woman should achieve complete chastity.'

"I did not exactly understand what he meant. I tried again to say something, but he interrupted me by abruptly standing on his feet and ending the conversation by saying, 'Daughter, we live this stupid life which is not worth living because we do not have the courage to leave it.' He then left me standing there in a state of utter perplexity and confusion."

After a period of silence Olga resumed her narrative. "My father now is in contact with some of those who are discontented with the present conditions in Russia. They dream of reform or a coup. He wrote to me that one of his colleagues, Vladimir, will pass through Paris on his way to London to attend a political conference. He urged me to be at his service. But what can I do? I hate politics and do not want to neglect my studies. Besides," she added, lowering her voice and her cheeks reddening, "why should I want to leave this green lawn, my friends the sparrows and these delightful moments?"

I said nothing while she was relating these things to me, my eyes resting on her white pure face and her very white hands. I avoided looking into her eyes which avoided my own. Not until the cool and humid air brushed against our faces and the time for the opening of the Art Academy drew near, did Olga offer me her white and delicate hand. I helped her to her feet. She tidied her shawl and wrapped it around her shoulders in a graceful feminine manner. We walked across the lawn, side by side, as we left the Luxembourg Garden.

Suddenly she interrupted my thoughts as if meaning to transfer both of us into a different atmosphere. She said, "How I like your friend Gibran. I admire his ambition to attain the highest goals. When he speaks it appears to me that I see a halo over his head. How I like to listen to him talk! His words are always graced by the touch of his beautiful soul. I wonder if there is a woman in his life? I mean there must be a woman in his life." She turned toward me as if she were awaiting an answer.

"Perhaps," I said, "very possibly. However, it is not my habit to intrude in his private life."

"You do the right thing," she said, "because a man's amorous affairs are exclusively his own."

We had reached the art book shop on the rue Vavin, so

we separated, and I continued walking to the Art Academy.

I spent two hours at the gallery painting. The model was as young as spring and naked like her mother Eve before enticed by the serpent to eat the apple. Every movement of her body spoke of beauty and overflowed with life. The artists around me looked at her with deep admiration. But what was wrong with me? Why did I find myself diverted from her and preoccupied only with the young woman with the white hands, fair face and blonde hair? Why was I so immersed in thoughts of Mademoiselle Olga, hearing every one of her words ringing in my ears, distracting me from concentrating on the naked model in front of me as if she were only a piece of stone?

"Count Leo used to put me on his knee and let me play with his beard;" "he is now in a state of war with his wife;" "man and woman should strive in their married life to attain complete chastity;" and, "I wonder if there is a woman in Gibran's life?"

CHAPTER SIX

SPRING STORM

☐ I left the Art Academy, walking towards the Dôme Café. There I found my friend Calmie with Dr. Casper, a young Belgian, who was studying bacteriology at the Pasteur Institute. Before long he got up, saying, "I leave you in each other's charge. I have a date."

"With a beautiful girl?"

"With a dying patient."

Outside a spring storm was raging. I didn't know what was on Calmie's mind when he turned to me and said, "Everybody carries a burden of worries on his own shoulders. But it seems to me that your burden is minimal. You walk with a light step and in an upright manner. Ah! Your paintings, where are they?"

I handed him several paintings which I had with me. He examined each one of them thoroughly and finally said, "These paintings are worth something. There is a demand for them." I replied, "I have several more of these paintings and I would like to put them in your charge."

Calmie answered, "You are a good soul, Yusuf, but you have no business sense." Both of us laughed and Calmie continued, "This morning your friend Gibran and I were visited by a movie producer who wanted to discuss his stories. Unfortunately, they were unsuitable for movie production. Gibran reminds me of myself ten years ago. Gibran has strong faith in himself, and he is sincere in his thinking. In his head there exists a vast and unlimited world which he wants to reveal to humanity. But do not forget, my friend, that we live in Paris, the

77

home of immortal literary masterpieces. It is not easy for a stranger who does not know the language to make a place for himself in the realm of Balzac, Flaubert, Zola, Anatole France and others."

I felt that it was my duty to defend Gibran and interrupted Calmie, saying, "But Gibran intends to exercise his art in the United States. This is what he is preparing for. He has friends there who appreciate his talent and who care about him. He knows English as if it were his native tongue, and therefore it is easy for him to get around in American society."

Ignoring me, Calmie said, "I have an idea. You and Gibran will be able to make piles of money, and right here in the heart of Paris. All you have to do is wear Oriental dress and a turban. Or, you could attempt to produce a kind of exotic and mysterious painting and have it advertised with the assistance of ladies and store managers who have experience in such things. The Parisian environment is now ripe for such things."

I asked, "Do I understand that you want us to practice humbuggery? God forbid, God forbid. I ask you, friend, not to repeat these 'excellent' suggestions anymore and especially not in Gibran's presence. However, let us now forget this matter. Tell me, how did you happen to come to Paris?" I asked him in a tone that sounded like an order.

Calmie answered readily, "When I was twenty and had finished my studies at the University of Bucharest, I developed a taste for art and fell in love with writing. I early achieved a measure of success which magnified the youthful hopes in my head—as would be natural for someone my age. I fell madly in love with a girl. She also loved me, and both of us thought that our happiness lay in getting married. But this was not to be, for we were soon confronted by reality. We were emphatically told that we could not marry because of the difference in our religions. I was a Jew and she was a Christian, the daughter of a priest. Finally, her people married her off, in spite of her protests, to a man whom she did not love. This shattered me. I almost lost my mind. From this terrible experience, I came to realize that anything that was not within the sphere of established custom was considered anathema by the majority of people. I counted these anathemas and found them to be endless. Humanity is drowned in them. Woe to him who attempts to endure the heavy yoke of differentness. Equal woe to him who tries to break this yoke while the tyrant holds the reins. Don't ask me how much I suffered from this crisis. But finally, I made an outline for a love story of radical content and suggested it to a publisher who after reading it, asked, aghast, 'Do you want to destroy me?' I wish that he had been satisfied with dampening my desire only, because then the whole episode would have ended at that point. But he betrayed me, informed the State censor of my work and took credit for foiling my 'criminal' actions. The news reached my rabbi and other religious leaders—who attempted to contact the Crown Prince Ferdinand and Princess Mary. It did no good, and my friends advised me to escape to Paris where my aunt and her children had taken refuge. She had fled there under similar circumstances in which her husband, the victim of ignorance and injustice, had died."

Here I interrupted Calmie, trying to assuage the sadness with which he was apparently filled. "You did well . . . Discretion is the better part of valor."

Outside, the storm became fierce. The cold wind furiously enveloped us whenever customers opened the door. Around us, hovering like sea gulls, looking for food were young poor girls. Finally Dr. Casper returned to tell us that the patient had passed away. He added after some thought, "The truth, friends, is that when man dies, he really dies. Life on this earth is nothing but a degeneration towards death." Then he asked me whether Mademoiselle Martine had dropped by the café. And when Calmie said that she had not, he sat there nervously swallowing a cup of warm onion soup. When finished, he hastily rose and left Calmie and me sitting in the warm corner of the café which, because of the bad weather, was empty.

Calmie said to me, "While we were leaving Gibran this

morning we saw a lady—I think she is American—going into his apartment. She entered as if going into her own house. A woman, my friend, is the only thing which can warm up the cold and desolate enviroment of man. Woe to the man whose home is not warmed by a woman."

I said, "It seems to me that you are feeling cold. Be sure, my friend, that the weather will calm down after the storm and sunny days and even very warm days will return."

Both of us turned toward the entrance, through which three girls, including Mademoiselle Martine, fluttered in like graceful swallows. Calmie called to her and revealed that Dr. Casper had inquired about her and that he seemed to be disturbed—gobbling down a cup of onion soup and hurriedly leaving the café. She said, "I too should like a warm cup of soup." Her friends expressed the same desire.

Calmie clapped his hands calling the waiter, and said loudly, "Bring us five cups of soup, a dish of fried potatoes and a bottle of red wine," adding in a low voice, "You only live once!"

How fast we became preoccupied with eating and drinking! Calmie began joking with the girls and I joined him. Then he moved on to the subject of the tragedy of life and I joined him in this too. Mademoiselle Martine, while the others were engaged in conversation, drew near to me and whispered in my ear, "Please, tell me frankly, does God exist, or not?"

I would have expected any question except that one, particularly in such circumstances and coming from the mouth of a Parisian girl. I did not know what to answer. She asked me again, persisting, "You know a lot of things, why don't you answer my question and perhaps quell some of the doubt that affects me? Is that too much trouble for you?"

I cautiously asked, "Have you asked your friend the doctor this question? He, too, has wide knowledge."

She said, "Yes, I have asked him. But one time he says that God exists and another time he says He does not." Calmie, hearing this part of our conversation, interjected himself, and, with a curious twitch of the eyebrows, said, "It is often the woman who makes man believe or not believe in the existence of God."

I continued, "Man can in fact feel the existence of God if he needs Him. He doesn't have to resort to theological or polemical arguments, which are often so complicated and abstract that they say and prove nothing at all. Kant has written eight hundred pages, Spinoza, I don't know how many hundreds of pages, and others wrote volumes to prove the existence of God. Nevertheless, doubt still disturbs the conscience of man and robs him of peace of mind."

"I wish I could know with certainty whether He exists or not," Mademoiselle Martine sobbed.

I said, attempting to comfort her, "Be sure, Mademoiselle, that God is everywhere. Everything testifies to His existence."

One of the young ladies concurred with my assurance nodding her head in approval. She said to Mademoiselle Martine in a triumphant voice, "Monsieur is right. Have not I told you that God exists?"

I don't think that anyone observing us, clustered in that warm corner, even if he were a prophet, could have guessed the subject of our discussion on that cold night at the Dôme Café . . . I really don't think so.

CHAPTER SEVEN

THE SYRIAC LANGUAGE

□ The next day when we were waiting for the model, Gibran asked, "Tell me what news do you have? Where were you last night when the storm raged over Paris?"

"I was buried in a warm corner of the Dôme Café with Calmie, Dr. Casper and some young ladies," I replied.

Gibran continued, "By the way, Calmie came to see me yesterday with a movie producer. It seems that my stories are not acceptable. As I understood it, they could not be readily adapted to film. Truthfully, Yusuf, I am not satisfied with what I have written up to now. I have tried to express some of my personal thoughts. But people seldom care for these, especially since they do not measure up to the level I seek. I am certain that I have something to tell people but my time has not yet come. What did Calmie and Dr. Casper tell you?"

"Many things", I replied, "including the telling of an emotional experience which befell Calmie and causes him to believe that one cannot with impunity challenge the canons of established custom. Dr. Casper was even more pessimistic. It is his belief that life on earth is nothing but degeneration and decay."

Gibran shook his head, "All of this could be true, but these attitudes are too lifeless, bleak and depressing. Man's life, Yusuf, is in need of beauty, happiness, poetry and love, without which man would become tired of life, hating it and even preferring death."

"Can you guess what one of the girls asked me?" I questioned. "She very seriously asked me whether or not God exists."

Gibran laughed, lit a cigarette, inhaled its smoke and puffed it off before he asked me, "And what answer did you give the girl? After all, your uncle is a Patriarch and you yourself understand divine matters." But before I could answer his question, he continued, analyzing the origin of religious beliefs, mentioning ancient gods and concluding that the majority of people have a God although there are many who doubt His existence. After an introspective pause, he said in a serious manner, "It is my intention to write about religion and religiousness."

I advised him not to waste his time with divine matters because many writers before him had written volumes about them and yet things remained the same. Every one on earth is satisfied with his own belief and with the religious instructions he received since childhood.

"Why do you," I asked him, "have so much desire to write?"

"Perhaps it is an instinct in me, Yusuf," he answered. "I remember when I began to doodle as children do; at that early age, I dreamt of selling my drawings for money. Likewise, whenever I read an interesting story, I felt a strong urge to write my own stories. Today, I still hope to make some money out of writing. Believe me when I say that I do not really become excited except when I draw or write."

For a joke, I told Gibran about Calmie's advice that we should wear Oriental dress and paint exotic pictures. Gibran objected vehemently, saying, "Nonsense! Humbuggery is not for us, Yusuf."

That morning the model did not show up. As Gibran was invited to lunch, I went alone to Madame Baudet's restaurant. In the evening, after I was through with my work at the Art Academy, I went to the Dôme Café. There I met Dr. Casper, who pointed his finger at me in a threatening manner and said, "Come, Monsieur Joseph, and sit next to me. I have been waiting for you. There is an account to settle between us. Why did you tell Martine that God exists?"

I thought that I had done something terrible. I mused to myself: Is it a crime if a young woman believes that

God exists? Is not this belief much better for her? Is there anything nicer than hearing a beautiful Parisian inquiring about divine matters?

"You are wrong, friend," I said aloud. "If you do not like to hear about this subject, stick to your microbes. It is, after all, your field of specialization and must undoubtedly be interesting."

Dr. Casper answered less enthusiastically than before, "The tragedy is those who exploit the idea of believing in God."

A loud noise which interrupted our conversation arose from the direction of the door. A group of friends entered and walked towards our table. They were Suzanne, Leah, Calmie and some other people I knew, including a stranger. The waiter came rushing over and added another table to ours. The circle became larger and I was introduced to the stranger. When he heard my name and noticed Leah repeat Gibran's words and hand gestures, "From there, from Lebanon, from near Jerusalem," he broadly smiled and said that he was extremely glad to meet a Lebanese. He added that he was from Prague, the capital of Bohemia, and that he was interested in the study of Oriental languages, particularly Syriac. He asked me if I knew this language. I told him that I did with a slight nod of the head and without much enthusiasm since my knowledge of the Syriac language was in reality rather limited. I had learned Syriac as a young boy in order to aid my grandfather, who is a priest, with the Mass. I used to repeat the words like a parrot without understanding their meaning.

The stranger showed great interest and asked me to utter a Syriac phrase in order to hear how it sounds. He leaned toward me attentively listening and the rest did the same. Even Suzanne and Leah were expectantly waiting to hear what I had to say. When I found myself the center of attention I began to recite, "*Men folutin dashmayo iro ishtadar*" ("From the court of heaven an angel was sent"). Leah could not help bursting out in her usual sarcastic laughter.

Calmie observed, "That sounds like Hebrew." As for

the Bohemian scholar, his eyes filled with tears of excitement and he requested me to repeat the phrase word for
word and repeated the words after me. Then he asked
me to recite another sentence, which I did, this time in a
louder voice: *"Al itre dbesme tobe bdehelthukh morie
ndabarayn wa bzadiquthe alifayn"* ("With the fragrance
of incense, lead me, O Lord in thy fear and teach me thy
righteousness.")

The group listened, impressed, while the aspiring
orientalist proceeded to explain that there is a tradition
among the Arabs, Jews, and the Fathers of the Church
that the Syriac language was the one spoken by Adam,
and that some scholars believe that the first version of the
Old Testament was written in Syriac, that Christ and His
disciples spoke this language, and finally, that the Maronites in Lebanon were still using Syriac in their church
rituals. He was on his way to the East to study certain ar-
chaeological excavations. He asked me to furnish him
with letters of recommendations to my friend, the Bishop
of Beirut, and another one to my uncle, the Patriarch of
the Maronites.

At this moment Mademoiselle Martine appeared at the
door. Dr. Casper got up, commenting, "Ah! Now I
understand why you support God and preach His existence to young women. You are related to Him." He bid
us goodby and left.

CHAPTER EIGHT

NIGHT EXCURSION

☐ Gibran entered the studio at the Art Academy carrying a folder of papers and his pens under his arm. He cast a long contemplative look at the naked young model lying on the stand looking bored and tired, and made a sign indicating that he was not pleased with what he saw. Seeing me across the room he approached, and whispered in my ear, "This poor girl provokes my pity. I have no desire to draw. I feel choked in this gloomy and depressing atmosphere. I prefer a walk along the river to watch the raging waters."

We left our papers and pens in the care of Madame Catherine who inquired worriedly if we did not like the model. She wished us a nice walk.

After ten minutes walk we reached Voltaire's statue. As we passed by Gibran exclaimed, "Here is your uncle the Patriarch of Ferney."

"Rather you should approach him and touch the hem of his dress in order that the blessings of humor might descend upon you, changing your gloomy demeanor," I retorted.

We stopped for a while to watch the waters roaring under the bridge and furiously splashing against the embankment. It was a formidable and revealing sight of the mighty powers of nature, and this power was augmented by the blackness of the night and the myriad faint lights dancing over the surface of the river in seeming defiance of the angry waves.

Gibran, whom I knew to be lost in thought, was the first to speak. He said, "Mademoiselle Olga came to see me this afternoon. She told me that the dampness caused by the rise of the river's water level was affecting the place in which she practices on the piano. She asked my permission to move the piano to my place. I don't think this is possible. The entrance to my place is narrow and besides, I usually receive friends and acquaintances in the afternoons. I believe that your place is more suitable because its entrance overlooks the street and you are not home most afternoons. As you know, Mademoiselle Olga is charming and educated and she would not cause you any trouble. I was not mistaken when I told you that she is decent and has noble character. Her profound education draws a great deal of admiration from me. She speaks English, German, French and Russian. She has told me about Tolstoy and Nietzsche and has expressed ideas, and made comments which have amazed me. How big is the difference between one woman and another. It even seems, sometimes, that they do not belong to the same human family."

We reached the Cathedral of Notre Dame and stopped for a moment in the square, admiring the entrance and the facade. It was utterly stupendous.

"This magnificent temple has been erected in honor of the patron of our country, Our Lady Mary," I remarked.

A young couple strolled by, holding hands, whispering and laughing. Gibran, forgetting Our Lady Mary, commented, "I wonder what they are talking about? Trivial matters no doubt, a syllable from the eternal song of life, a mere prelude to the deeper intoxications of love. But when infatuation dies down, quarrels begin, followed by separation. Perhaps the outcome of their love will be a new child which would then grow to repeat the eternal drama—a slight ripple on the surface of the ocean of existence."

We had reached the old streets of Paris behind the Church of St. Julian the Mendicant. Gibran asked me, "I wonder what this saint accomplished?"

I replied, "Do you mean Julian the Mendicant? I don't know exactly what he accomplished except that he died a martyr. But I do know something of what Julian the Apostate, the Roman emperor, did."

"You sympathize more with heretics than with saints," Gibran commented. "At least it seems like that to me. Come on, tell me what your friend the heretic did."

I said, "First of all he loved to live in Paris. Like us, he was a man of taste. Furthermore, he tried to correct the mistakes of his uncle, the emperor Constantine, and restore the temples and glory of the ancient gods. He happened to make Paris his capital instead of Constantinople in order to be far removed from the East where doctrinal disputes developed and spread quickly."

Here, Gibran changed the subject as if satisfied with what had been said. He began to relate some droll stories about Balzac and how he roamed these streets in the dark nights picking up impressions in order to incorporate them into his stories. Indeed, every one of these streets, every door and window and every passing shadow can inspire reflections about the tragedy of life, its irony, beauty and ugliness.

And then Gibran transferred to his own inner and mysterious world, asking, "And we, who are we? Where did we come from and where are we going? We are like wandering shadows in these narrow alleys while at a short distance away in the spacious streets flows the stream of mankind, whose members, one by one, sooner or later disappear. Strange is this life; who can know its secrets and predict its final ends?"

I cannot remember every word Gibran said during that night excursion. But I can well remember his state of mind. His body, which he moved slowly over the damp ground, was a burden to his soaring soul and the metaphysical source of his thoughts.

We had reached the Sorbonne. I stopped in front of the statue standing in the middle of a small garden. I raised my hat in a salute and told Gibran, "This is the great poet Dante who visited Paris at the beginning of the fourteenth century. His many admirers built this statue."

"How far did you get in translating *The Divine Comedy*? Many times you have promised to read some parts of it to me and I can think of no better time for this than tonight. What do you say?"

I liked Gibran's suggestion and we went to my place. In order to get there quickly, we took the tram to Denver Square, and on the way I explained why Dante was such a great poet.

I said, "Dante ranks third after Homer and Virgil, perhaps even surpassing them. He is the first modern writer. He left no emotion unplumbed or theme unexamined. And thus he did this with the utmost eloquence and profundity. He had loved Beatrice since he was ten years old and she a little younger. But death snatched her away when she was barely twenty. Later, Dante was exiled for political reasons and lived the rest of his days far from his beloved city, Florence. One day he sighed in agony and from the depths of his soul cried out, 'Oh how difficult it is to walk in and out of strangers' homes without ever entering my own home!' Nevertheless, Dante sang immortal songs which ensured his place amongst the greatest poets. He never forgot his love for Beatrice who became, in *The Divine Comedy*, his faithful guide on his journey through heaven. Some maintain that she alone inspired his poetry and her living memory was the constant fountain of his inspiration."

Looking as if he were enjoying my little talk about Dante, Gibran interrupted me, saying, "How I would love to visit Florence and walk in the streets of Dante, Giotto, Angelico, Botticelli, Leonardo, Michelangelo, Machiavelli and many others who lived and worked in that city. I shall eternally grieve if I am denied the opportunity to climb to the top of Fiesole."

At this moment we reached my residence. Gibran asked me, "Is there anything to eat? Talking about poetry will not fill the stomach."

When we were inside I gave him some yogurt, jam and a box of cookies. I also boiled two cups of coffee. After eating, we sat on the divan and while Gibran listened,

90

resting his head on his shoulder, I read the translation of the fifth canto to him, in which Dante discusses love.

I repeated some phrases in Italian for the sake of clarity. I raised my voice when I came to a dramatic passage until I reached the last part where Dante says, "And I dropped like a dead body." I turned toward Gibran to see the effect my reading had on him, and there he was, with his head downward and his eyes wet with tears. I could not help but laugh loudly which snapped him out of his reverie. He asked me why I had laughed.

I replied, "I feel like laughing."

Gibran immediately answered, "And I feel like going to bed. It is too late to go home, so I shall sleep on your divan." He took off his shoes and suit-jacket, stretched out and went to sleep.

It was truly a simple life that we lived in Paris. Later, in one of his letters to me from Boston, Gibran reminisced,

> Every evening my soul returns to Paris and wings among its places. And every morning I wake up thinking of those days which we spent among the temples of art and the valleys of dreams.

In the meantime, Mademoiselle Olga moved her piano to my place. We agreed that she should be able to practice alone in the afternoons and I gave her the key. She was immensely relieved and soon became delighted with her new surroundings of paintings, books and flowers. She practiced seriously and long and from time to time she invited me and Gibran to listen to the music of Beethoven and Tchaikovsky. The Russian samover was always boiling with hot water for tea. We brought biscuits and candy with us and sat sipping tea and discussing diverse subjects. There was nothing to disturb our happy friendship. Mademoiselle Olga presented each one of us with brocaded Russian hats made of black velvet which we ostentatiously wore on our night excursions.

CHAPTER NINE

MADAME BAUDET'S RESTAURANT

☐ Georgette told us, while serving us lunch, that she was intending to leave the small restaurant near the Luxembourg Garden to work at Madame Baudet's restaurant located where the boulevard Raspail meets the rue Léopold Robert. I discussed the matter with Gibran and we decided that the new restaurant was agreeable to both of us. It was half way between our residences and also close to free art academies.

Madame Baudet's restaurant was the first in the Latin Quarter to be built in the modern style. It was different from the classical style which was still popular then. Instead of being straight and plain, the wooden frames, the manageress' desk, the doors and the windows all had curved lines ending in something similar to the shape of big leaves. Furthermore, it had many unusual decorations which were undoubtedly inspired by the new trend in art.

Since the beginning of the summer, the tables were set on the wide sidewalk in front of the restaurant, surrounded by plants and flowers.

As to Madame Baudet's dress, it was not touched by this revolution. She had preserved a pure classical style. At the age of fifty, she had a full forehead, and a round face encompassed by white hair severely combed back. Her eyes were sharp as those of an eagle, especially when she noticed something that had to be done by one of her employees.

When Gibran and I passed by, greeting her with respect, she smiled with motherly affection—which was no wonder, because we were prominent customers. While regular customers paid five centimes as a tip, we paid ten. The waitresses whispered to each other that we were princes from Lebanon. Whenever Georgette saw us coming in she would hurry to reserve the best table for us and draw our attention to the best dishes on the menu. She treated us differently than other customers and we enjoyed this special treatment. It made us feel more important than the others. The price of a meal in those days, including the best dishes, was no more than two francs.

Thus, we were treated with respect and honor at Madame Baudet's restaurant. We sat in it like princes and conversed as we wished, covering topics than ran from great hopes to trivial matters.

Sometimes, when we felt no great desire to work at the Art Academy, and when Gibran had no appointments, we liked to stroll on the boulevard Montparnasse until we reached the corner where the Café du Lilas stood. There we drank a cup of coffee, admiring the statue of Marshal Ney pointing his sword forward. It was made by the sculptor Rudé. Then we would venture to the Jardin Observatoire, walking around the beautiful pond and gaping like astonished children at the statues of the four continents, by the sculptor Carpaux. Each one of these statues was of a woman representing a continent. All of them were naked and beautiful as they supported, over their heads, the round globe of the earth.

It was truly a masterpeice of art. Around these statues water gushed from every direction. The evergreen trees shaded both sides of the wide road. No taste surpasses that of the French. "We are in Paris!" Gibran used to exclaim from excessive joy.

Now when I close my eyes, how quickly the memory of Gibran comes to my mind—his affectionate smile, warm voice, and expressive hands. I can see us walking to the Luxembourg Garden, turning left and sitting on the roof which overlooks the Palace and a part of the garden. I can hear the echo of Gibran's voice in my ear, "We are in Paris, Yusuf! In this rich garden and on this road stretching before us walked many great learned men and artists. I can feel the presence of Puvis de Chavannes, Carriére, Balzac, Alfred de Musset, Victor Hugo, Pasteur, Curie, Taine and Renan. I feel as if I can trace their footprints on this road."

I had then commented, "And those young women who are the the source of inspiration, do not traces of their delicate feet appear to you on the road? The feet of Mademoiselle Olga for instance?"

Gibran softly smiled, his eyes half closed, and I left him with his thoughts of great men while I turned to thoughts of those young women who are the source of all inspiration.

After a long silence, Gibran asked me, "How about visiting Lady Genevieve as long as we are near? I have not seen her for a long time and I would like to see her."

It did not take us long to leave the garden and walk toward la rue Soufflot until the outline of the Pantheon—which Soufflot built before the Revolution—appeared before our eyes. My God! How could a temple stand on top of another one with a dome perching on top of both of them?

On the ruins of the ancient church of St. Genevieve this temple was built in honor of the patroness of the people of Paris. During the great Revolution it was converted into a mausoleum for illustrious men and renamed the Pantheon. On its facade was inscribed the following: "The Country Thanks Its Great Men." After the Revolution it was turned once more into a church. The Republic had recently made it again a mausoleum. We entered it.

The first thing we saw was the painting of St. Genevieve by Puvis de Chavannes which Gibran admired tremendously. She is standing, in this painting, on a balcony in front of her room. Her head is covered with a white shawl and she is holding its ends with one hand while the

95

other is resting upon the wall. As a sentinel in the moonlight, she is watching over the sleeping city and its people. It is, indeed, an immortal masterpiece of art.

It is this woman who calmed down the terrorstricken people of Paris as the barbarian hordes of Attila approached the city in the middle of the fifth century, having swept through most of Europe leaving death and desolation in their wake. He reached the very gates of Paris and stood before its walls. Genevieve went out to meet him face to face. What did she tell him? What language did she speak? What was the tone of her voice? What appearance did she present that persuaded the formidable Attila to turn back and leave Paris?

Gibran asked passionately, "Is there a deeper and more solemn tranquility than that which appears on her face?" I concurred with Gibran's words by shaking my head in approval, and with my eyes still fixed on the painting I said, "A painting should be either this way or never."

Then we moved to look at a second painting representing the death of the saint while she was blessing those present. It is the work of Jean Paul Laurence. This painting was classical in the strictest sense. It is cold, even boring and it has no spirit.

Gibran remarked, "As I have told you many times, Yusuf, I do not like the art of Laurence. Sometimes I even hate it. I would like to be free to develop my own kind of art."

We heard the guide saying loudly, "The door to the crypt is open. Who wants to visit the crypt?"

We descended to the crypt with the others. The guide stood on a small podium and pointed his finger towards a tomb, saying like a parrot, "Here lies Voltaire, a great philosopher, a great writer and a great poet." Then he pointed to another grave and said, "Here lies Jean Jacques Rousseau, a great writer and thinker." He pointed to yet another grave and said, "Here lies Victor Hugo, a great poet."

Gibran pressed my arm and whispered to me, "I have had enough of greatness. I prefer a walk along the river."

"You are right. Let's go," I agreed.

We slipped slowly out of the crowd, and ascended the steps onto the boulevard St. Michel on the river's side. At first we looked at books and paintings in the windows and then, while walking down the boulevard, Gibran began to talk about eminent writers and the role they played in awakening their countries. He said, "Voltaire and Rousseau were the conscience of France toward the end of the eighteenth century. No wonder that they rest in peace under the dome of the Pantheon."

I asked him, "But do you know what Louis XVI said about them?"

"You mean that Bourbon who was sent to the guillotine by the men of the Revolution?" he asked.

"Yes, he himself," I replied. "When he was on trial in the Palace of Justice, seeing nearby some of Voltaire and Rousseau's books, he uttered with contempt, 'These two men have destroyed France!'"

"He actually meant the Bourbon monarchy, of course. Napoleon once said, 'If the Bourbons had kept a watchful eye on literary activity, their star would have never set so soon! Voltaire and Rousseau were not that great, but their contemporaries were small.'"

"This is true," said Gibran, "there is no doubt that books influence and shape the lives of nations. Writers and intellectuals stimulate people to think. It is with Voltaire and Rousseau that France began to think—even Napoleon could not stop it from thinking. I wonder when this miracle of thinking will happen in the East? And when and with whom the East will begin to think?"

"With Gibran!" I exclaimed with enthusiasm. But Gibran stared at me and imagined I was mocking him. "Yes! With Gibran the East will begin to think," he exclaimed.

"And his countrymen will build him a very lofty Pantheon," I added.

We had reached the bank of the Seine where books were exhibited on stands along the embankment.

CHAPTER TEN

MADEMOISELLE MARTINE

□ I do not want the reader to think that Gibran and I were always in each other's company. Often, more than a week passed before we saw each other. When we finally did meet, Gibran used to ask me, "Where were you hiding all this time? How are the young women of the Parish?"

I replied, "They are in good health and inquire about yours."

Although our walks together were the most enjoyable part of our stay in Paris, I often walked alone along the Seine. I enjoyed walking through the narrow alleys behind the Academie Francaise and then strolling on the rue Seine which was quiet and far removed from the noise of the street traffic. Or, I would go to the street next to the Theatré Odeon where there was a book shop containing many modern works. After spending a moment there, looking at the books, I would walk toward the Luxembourg Gardens, finally reaching the Jardin Observatoire at whose end there was a beautiful pond. There I never became tired of looking at the four naked beauties holding the earth aloft.

One day, while I was looking at them, oblivious of my surroundings, I heard a voice say to me, "How strange you are! You let brass beauties divert you from the human ones." I turned to see three beautiful young women laughing flirtatiously. They were Mademoiselle

Martine and two of her friends. I do not know which of them was most beautiful, but they were so beautiful that I shouted to myself, "O, St. Antonius! how plentiful are those beauties who are the source of inspiration."

Mademoiselle Martine asked me to join her at the Café du Lilas in an hour because she had something to tell me. I accepted her invitation. When I got there, knowing what was on her mind, I opened the conversation by asking, "Do you still desire to know whether God exists or not?"

"That is right, Monsieur," she replied.

"I have told you that He exists everywhere although He is invisible," I explained.

"Thank you, Monsieur. But please tell me," she asked, suddenly changing the subject, "who is that person standing on the pedestal with his sword pointed forward?"

"It is the statue of Marshal Ney, one of Napoleon's commanders," I replied.

"But why is his statue here?" she further questioned.

I explained, "After the Emperor abdicated and the monarchy was restored to France, Ney swore his allegiance to the King. But, when the Emperor came once more to power, Ney renewed his allegiance to him. When the King regained his throne once again, he sentenced Ney to death. It was in this very spot that the bullets of a firing squad tore through the chest of the valiant soldier."

"Did this happen long ago?" she asked.

"About a hundred years ago," I replied.

We were sitting at a small table under the shade of a tree. I ordered two cups of coffee. Mademoiselle Martine returned once again to the original subject.

She began, "If God does exist and He will judge us in the next world for everything that we have done . . ."

"I told you, Mademoiselle," I interrupted, "that God is great and He is tolerant and forgiving, and besides He has a good heart," I assured her.

"I may as well tell you, I would like to marry according to religious law. I hate being a mistress," she confessed.

"You are right in your attitude," I said. "Do not let anything else influence you even if God does not exist."

"The Doctor . . . all that he cares for is a woman, with or without laws," she complained.

"This is the fashion today with those who do not believe that He exists," I said. "Most men, Mademoiselle, are selfish, liars, dishonest, cowardly . . ." and I went on to the end of Voltaire's diatribe which I had memorized in order to quote whenever needed.

"True, true," Mademoiselle Martine sighed deeply.

"Do you not have a family or relatives, Mademoiselle?" I asked.

"Yes," she answered. "My father works as a signal man at the railway station. My mother cooks for him, washes his clothes and quarrels with him, only to once again reconcile with him. Of course, they embrace each other and the result is always another brother or sister. I am the third of eight children. My elder brother is in the army in Indochina."

"Get to the point," I interrupted. "How old are you and how did you live up until now and how did you come to know the Doctor?"

"I am twenty-two," she replied. "I spent three years with a certain family, helping the wife and taking care of the children. A few months ago while I was going to the Bon Marché to buy something it began to rain. All of a sudden, someone opened an umbrella and covered my head. It was Dr. Casper who accompanied me to the entrance of the store. I thanked him and went in. But I was very surprised to see him still waiting for me when I left the store. He walked with me and asked me when I was free. I said, 'On Saturday.' He said that he would wait for me Saturday afternoon at the entrance of the Luxembourg Gardens near the museum. All week long I was torn with conflict. I swore to myself that I would not keep the date. How could I go out with a man whom I hardly knew? However, when Saturday came I found myself wearing my best dress and hurrying to meet him."

"There is nothing extraordinary about this story," I observed. "What I would like to know is why are you so preoccupied with the problem of whether God exists or not?"

"I told you that my purpose in life is to marry according to religious law. I want to have a Christian husband and children. This morning I saw a bride holding the hand of her bridegroom as they left a church. They were radiant with happiness. How beautiful the bride looked in her white satin dress and large transparent veil! I was so moved that I cried."

At this point, she actually began dabbing at her eyes. I felt sorry for her and tried to comfort her. I said, "There is too great a difference between you and the Doctor. It would be better if you looked for a man of your own social class."

It appears that she did not like my comment for she bluntly answered, "I know a poor girl who married a rich man. In the beginning, he loved her even though he was hesitant to marry her. Afraid that she might lose him, she submitted to him and he finally married her."

"This could happen," I said, "but it is not a good example for you to follow. The girl should stay in the care of her parents, and should be guided by them. She should follow her parents' advice until the right man comes by to marry her."

"But going back to my parents is not possible," she objected.

"You should then pray," I replied, "and pray fervently, asking God to help you and solve your problem. Although God is busy with the universe, if you prayed to him fervently and with faith He would undoubtedly answer a beautiful Parisian like yourself."

And then I inquired, "Does the Doctor love you?"

"I do not know," she replied.

"Do you love him?" I inquired.

"I do not know that either," she said.

"Sorry," I said, "it is time to go to the Art Academy."

"I will walk with you up to the Dôme Café," she said.
On the way, and after a short silence, she implored me
to help her, saying, "The Doctor says that you are his
dearest friend. May God bless you and reward you."

CHAPTER ELEVEN

DR. CASPER'S IDEAS

☐ One day at noon Dr. Casper entered Madame Baudet's restaurant. When he saw me and Gibran eating lunch he waved to us and we motioned to him to join us. When he had finished his meal the three of us entered into a discussion about science.

I remember how the Doctor spoke convincingly and with authority about the latest scientific developments in medicine and astronomy. He reviewed the history of science from ancient times until the end of the eighteenth century—a century which saw a formidable material and spiritual revolution. He mentioned the reply that Le Place had given to Napoleon upon the presentation of his book, containing his theory of astronomy, to the then First Consul. After congratulating him on his magnificent book, Napoleon had asked him: "Newton mentioned God in his book many times while you did not mention Him once——why?"

Le Place replied, "Because I have no need for an illusion such as that."

"Illusion?" Gibran objected vehemently; and he began to present philosophical arguments by beginning, "Nothing comes from nothing."

At this the Doctor interrupted, "You are indulging in useless justifications, my friend. They are meaningless. Science has the ability to explain and prove everything. I will not bow my head except to science."

Gibran became furious and said, "The intellect of man is limited."

But the Doctor raised his voice even louder, shouting,

"You Easterners have bequeathed to the world beliefs which mislead sound minds." Then he turned to me and said accusingly, "And you have mislead Mademoiselle Martine by telling her that God exists."

I defended myself by saying in a joking manner, "It is you who have misled the poor young woman by telling her that God does not exist. Martine wants to marry according to the laws of man and God while you are an unprincipled and disbelieving scoundrel who does not care for laws."

The Doctor raised his fist to me in a threatening gesture and laughingly said, as if he had lost the round, "You Easterners!"

I did the same, raising my fist higher than his, and retorted, "Rather, you Westerners!"

We all laughed and Gibran said in his usual solemn manner, "Wise up fellows, enough childishness."

While we were thus engaged Georgette returned with a dish of fruits. She smiled when she saw us laughing and commented, "It warms my heart to see you this way. The blood of youth is hot in your veins. While you live, others sleep or sulk or exist as if they were sentenced to hard labor."

After lunch, our friend the Doctor invited us to visit the Pasteur Institute where he was doing research related to microbes. We accepted the invitation with pleasure and happily went with him since we had long desired to make such a visit.

At first sight, the Pasteur Institute appears to the visitor like a city within a city. It was the domain of Dr. Casper where he moved with assurity and spoke with authority. Neither Gibran nor I said a word in opposition to him.

The Doctor explained, "All of these animals—horses, cattle, rabbits, chicken and mice are used for experiments."

Gibran remarked, "Every being in this world has its own role. What do these beasts care except to eat and drink? Does it occur to them, I wonder, that they are rendering invaluable service to mankind?"

The Doctor continued, "And here is the library. Here

are medical publications and scientific reports in all languages from all over the world—except from the East. The East does not even know that we exist." He then asked sarcastically, "Do you have doctors in your country?"

"Our ancestors invented medicine in ancient times," I retorted angrily.

"Our ancestors, our ancestors . . . what about you yourselves? We want to know what you have and what you have invented," he replied.

Then he went back to explaining things. "These bottles are used to store microbes. In them we observe and study their nature, development and life. We search for drugs to combat them. These are the microbes of the plague, syphilis, tuberculosis and others, and here are their magnified pictures. They are of different forms and shapes as you see. Each one of them enters the human body and bloodstream in its own way. Through our study, research and experiments we seek for the means to combat them. It was Pasteur and Koch who opened the way for us to do this."

We continued our guided tour for an hour or so, during which time we learned many interesting things. Before leaving I asked the Doctor at the door in a serious tone, "And what about the umbrella which you raise over the heads of young women when it rains?"

He raised his fist to my face and said, laughing, "I will give you a similar umbrella as a present."

"Thank you very much," I said.

On the street and as soon as we were out of the Doctor's sight, Gibran asked me, "What is the story of the umbrella to which you alluded and over which you and the Doctor laughed?"

"It is a trap for young women," I remarked.

"What! A trap for young women? How can you be so flippant! Is this all that you have learned from the Doctor's lecture? Have not you observed that the world of science goes beyond and surpasses the world of art?"

I replied, having resumed my seriousness, "The worlds of science and art are the foundations of human civilization. They support and compliment each other, but the true key to success and fulfillment is in doing a good job."

"Yes," said Gibran, "the European man does a good job. The word 'can't' is unknown to him. Our friend the Doctor, for example, earnestly approaches his work and is concerned with knowing all he can about science. As to his revolutionary ideas and principles, they are his own business. Nevertheless, I like to listen to him speak. His words are as lively as a burning fire."

"Yes! All of his speeches are full of life," I agreed. "I have never heard a better speaker in my life."

I added, "I have told you many times, Gibran, that the Dôme Café is like a 'popular academy' for the understanding of life and the universe. Too bad you do not like its atmosphere."

"Its disadvantages outweigh its advantages," Gibran ironically replied. "It would be unbearable if it were not for Leah and Suzanne."

We approached my residence and heard music coming from inside. Gibran looked at me, "Do you hear the music? It is Olga playing the piano. I almost forgot that she was coming to play for us."

"I did not forget," I replied, "and to prove it, I have brought some sweets from Bochnet's store."

After greeting Olga she suggested, "Before enjoying your tea and sweets, I want you to listen to a sonata by Beethoven. While rehearsing it I thought of my special friends, and here they are in person."

"They are also here in mind, body and soul," I added.

We sat on the divan in the dimly lit room listening to the sweet melodies surging out of the piano, Gibran resting his head on his hand and both of us dreaming.

In my own fantasies I was seeing now the paintings of Michelangelo move and dance on the ceiling, now the souls of the tormented in Dante's *Inferno* writhe and sink in fire, and now the spring nymphs of Botticelli dance on the green lawn.

"What are you dreaming about, Gibran?" I asked.

"I am intoxicated, Yusuf," Gibran murmured. "The

cedar mountains appear before my eyes, the holy valley, the winter storm and flowers of the spring. Ah! Who will carry me on a magic carpet to Bsharri?"

Thus we expressed our feelings while listening to Beethoven's sonata.

While once again deep in contemplation we heard Olga say, "And now listen to this concerto which is the last piece I shall play."

"Is it true that it will be the last?" Gibran asked jokingly. I was surprised, for such a question was contrary to Gibran's nature.

We began to sip tea and make conversation. The following dialogue took place between Olga and Gibran:

"He who does not have a taste for music has no taste at all."

"In order to understand a piece of serious music we should listen to it many times exactly as we do with a poem or a literary piece in order to thoroughly absorb it and understand it."

"The ancient Greeks began the education of their children by teaching them music before the sciences. They believed that music trained the character and taught order."

"One day King Philip of Macedonia entered the hall where his son Alexander was playing the harp. He was astonished by his skillful playing and reproached him: 'Are you not ashamed to play with such skill?' Perhaps the King was afraid that music would distract his son from the responsibility of kingship as well as from the philosophy of Aristotle, the secrets of which involve a great deal of effort to master."

I finally interposed, "In my opinion art, like philosophy, helps to emancipate the intellect and soul of man."

Olga asked me to elaborate on what I meant. I complied by saying, "The masterpieces of sculpture, painting and music are like literary masterpieces in that they nourish our beings and help us create a vision particularly our own, of life and the universe. They stimulate us to think and work and elevate us above the lower animals and bring us closer to the realm of the gods. Those who are untouched by the graces of art and philosophy are handicapped. They are like cripples who try in vain to rise and march with the stream of true civilization."

I spoke spontaneously and enthusiastically shifting my eyes between Olga and Gibran. I became even more enthusiastic when I saw they appreciated what I had said. I continued, "If I may define human civilization in a nutshell, I would say that it is a statue, a painting, a melody or a poem. Through them we can perceive the powers which move the universe and understand the essence of things and events. They reflect and reveal the life of the shepherd kings in the stone age, the hold of the magi, the cruelty of the Assyrian kings, the religious profundity of the ancient Egyptians, the brilliance of the ancient Greeks and the Renaissance Italians."

"And of this present time as well," interrupted Gibran.

"The present time," I replied, "is lost in anarchy and in crazy useless pursuits."

Olga turned to Gibran and changed the conversation into English as if she wanted, for some private reason, to preclude my participating in their conversation. Then she got up, picked up her things and made ready to leave. Gibran told me in a low voice in Arabic, "Where did you get all of this eloquence, you devil? Could it have been inspired by her?"

"Does she not deserve even more than that?" I asked.

"She told me that she admires you," Gibran teased.

In this manner our conversation went on, our emotions coursing through our spiritual veins like demonic microbes laboring in secret hoping not to be detected.

CHAPTER TWELVE

MADEMOISELLE ROSINA

☐ I went to see Gibran and found him as usual sitting at his desk with a cup of coffee and the ever-burning cigarette whose smoke lazily wound upward in curls disappearing in the room's atmosphere. He had a pen in his hand, writing and then erasing what he had written. He turned to me with dream-like eyes and, seemingly cheered up by my presence, began to chant to himself, " 'Oh, Gibran, why are you so silent? What has happened to you that you have neglected inkpots and writing?' " And then he added with a thin smile of satisfaction that was mingled with anxiety, "This is what an Egyptian poet whom I don't know has written to me.

"The people, Yusuf, demand to hear something new from me. I have, as you know, precious treasures. How wonderful it would be if words obeyed my will; look." He handed me a paper covered from top to bottom with frantic erasures, except for certain incomplete phrases which survived here and there, such as "when I came of age", "at the age of twenty" and "when I opened my eyes to the light".

I looked at him and saw a very ambitious artist and poet with little means, dissatisfied with his condition and with the world.

"Have patience, Gibran, and stop worrying," I reassured him. "Who told you that reform cannot be achieved except by writing? Who told you that art is not a more powerful catalyst than words? How much safer it would be, Gibran, if we tried to hold only one apple in our hand at a time."

111

After a moment I changed the subject. "Get ready; I have a cheerful surprise for you. Within a few minutes one of Botticelli's nymphs will be here. She is a nice young Italian woman whom I met last evening at the Art Academy. She is gorgeous. You will definitely like her. Where are the paints?"

As we prepared to meet the new guest there was a slight knock at the door. A Madonna entered wearing a simple green dress and a red shawl over her head. In her hand was my note containing Gibran's address. I began the introduction: "This is Monsieur Gibran."

"And, this is Rosina," she interrupted.

Rosina removed the shawl to reveal glowing, long golden hair. Gibran was astonished and his eyes fixed upon her. He whispered in Arabic, "My eyes have never seen more beautiful hair."

"You have yet to see the most beautiful female body. Rosina, take off your clothes," I told the young woman in Italian.

Without embarrassment Rosina took off her clothes. She turned to us asking the familiar question, "What position do you want me to take?"

Gibran took a long time before he answered, "You look as if you are floating in the air, Mademoiselle, carried on angels' arms toward heaven." He directed Rosina to a stand covered with a rug and several pillows. There, Rosina lay on her back, raising slightly her left side and right arm. Gibran supported her with pillows, muttering in Arabic, "Here are the angels; I wish I were one of them." Then he added in French, "Are you comfortable, Mademoiselle?"

"Yes, thank you," she said. She asked me in Italian, "What language does your friend speak?"

"Lebanese," I said.

She thought I said "Japanese" and inquired, "Are you Japanese?"

"Yes," I said.

At this point the introduction ended and Gibran and I became occupied with drawing the body of the beautiful young woman carried on angels' arms. Gibran sometimes spoke loudly and sometimes muttered to himself: "Why are you so silent, Gibran?" Rosina looked sometimes at me and other times at Gibran until finally she became drowsy. She dropped her head a little and a few locks of her hair flowed gracefully on her shoulders in an unsurpassed scene of beauty and charm.

An atmosphere of solemn silence overwhelmed us in the face of this virgin and pure beauty. The forty-eight minutes assigned for her sitting passed all too quickly. It was time to rest. Gibran asked Rosina whether she wanted to rest. She contentedly answered without opening her eyes, "Is there any more rest than this? Continue working."

Once more our brushes dipped into paint seeking inspiration from the naked beauty of those pure and divine moments. Gibran, thinking hard and never lifting his eyes from that reposeful body, commented, "If only my fingers would obey my mind and feeling, Gibran should then create wonders."

Then he asked, "What do you know about this girl, Yusuf?"

I said, "I met her yesterday at the Academy and admired her body. At the end of the sitting a few artists asked her if she were free the next day. She shook her head indicating that she was not. I knew that she was Italian. I approached her and placed a franc in her hand asking her in her own language whether she was free. Her eyes brightened and she answered, 'Just for one day.' Perhaps she wanted to give it a try. Then I gave her your address."

After a while Gibran said in his deep voice, "Who knows, maybe this girl is in need of our protection and assistance. Paris is full of danger, especially for helpless young women."

During that period of his life Gibran was under the influence of a mental condition which I called "Franciscanism". His greatest concern was to reform the world, protect the weak and express the most profound human sentiments such as nobility and honor.

The sitting ended and Gibran paid Rosina two and

one-half francs. It was his turn, that day, to pay the model. While Rosina dressed Gibran noticed that the small metal crucifix around her neck was hung on a string and that her black clumsy peasant shoes were unsuited to her very white feet. He whispered to me, "Look at her. She is poor."

Then he asked her politely whether she was free next week, but she hesitated to answer. Just then, loud knocking was heard at the door. Turning to me, Gibran said, "You understand her language. You arrange the matter with her. We need four or five sessions." He went to open the door and returned holding the arm of a Mrs. Hamilton who examined Rosina from top to bottom while Rosina did the same. The American lady began busily talking to Gibran in English, and Rosina took leave without telling us whether she would be free.

This famous writer had come to invite us to lunch and to an afternoon party which might be attended by Auguste Rodin. As I knew no English, I did not exactly relish an American social gathering, and furthermore, I did not care to be introduced to Rodin. I excused myself and walked toward the door. Gibran bid me good-by and said, "I shall be at your place tomorrow around five o'clock. Give my regards to Mademoiselle Olga."

After walking a few steps on the Boulevard Raspail, I spied Rosina walking ahead of me. She tarried a little in front of a shoe store, and then approached an old woman sitting on a sidewalk seat and placed money in her hand. A young man passed by and whispered something in Rosina's ear which made her turn away from him and walk toward the intersection. Presently, I reached her and queried in Italian, "Where are you going? Give me your hand to help you walk." She was frightened at first, but when she recognized me she offered me her hand.

She said, "I am going to a place near the Parc Montsouris, about a half-hour's walk from here. And where are you going?"

"To Madame Baudet's restaurant at the corner of the street," I said. "Is anyone waiting for you?"

She said, "No."

I said, "Would you accept my invitation?"

"Happily. I am starving," she said.

As we sat at the table she loosened up a bit and she began to relate her story to me. She told me that her family lived in an Italian village called Anticoli and that she began her career by going to Rome in the winter to sit for artists. But she was told that the opportunities were greater in Paris, and she, with her three brothers who are construction workers, moved there. At this point, it became difficult for her to continue, but she went on, "I wish I had not come to Paris. I feel like a stranger here. I have no mother, no sisters, and no . . ."

"What about your brothers?" I remarked.

She said, "My brothers are busy working. They are cruel to me and do not understand me. They take all the money I make." Tears flowed down her cheeks.

I said, "Do you always find work when there are so many young Parisian women available?"

She said, "I do not find it very difficult. Whenever I sat at the Academy for an artist I always got plenty of offers. However, I don't agree to sit for an artist unless I approve of the way he looks."

I wanted to assuage her melancholy and, smiling, I asked her, "How did you like my looks as well as those of Gibran?"

But she did not answer my silly question and continued, saying, "And when I don't find work, the door of the 'old satyr' is always open."

"The old satyr?" I repeated, puzzled.

"Yes, Master Rodin," she said.

I gasped when I heard the name and gently reminded Rosina, "You know, Mademoiselle, Master Rodin is the prince of artists. Why do you call him a satyr?"

She smiled and said, "When I first went to his studio with a friend he approached me and felt my shoulders and chest and asked me while rubbing his chin like a satyr whether I were still a virgin. I took his question as an insult and attempted to leave. But he stopped me and began laughing to himself."

"And what happened after that?" I asked.

"Well, there were three naked young women in his studio frolicking and laughing. Master Rodin told me and my friend, 'Do the same as they are doing. Eat chocolate whenever you like.' He showed us a box of expensive candies which was on a table. He sat and worked while we played and ate chocolate, not knowing which one of us he was drawing. From time to time he called on us to move about and not remain stationary."

I said to Rosina, "The artist always needs to see naked bodies in motion. Art lovers, Mademoiselle, vie to buy his works for high prices. Furthermore, his works occupy first place in museums."

Rosina shrugged her shoulders, unimpressed. She continued with less enthusiasm, "A woman came to see him like the one who came to see your friend. She wore a big hat with a bird on top and a long dress with a hem she had raised by hand. She wore high-heeled shoes and spoke a language which I didn't understand. Immediately Rodin paid each one of us five francs, serving notice that our assignment had ended."

I emphasized, "Rodin is a great and rich artist. His works bring him a great deal of fame and money." To change the subject, I asked Rosina if she could dance and sing.

Her eyes brightened and she answered with guileless joy, "My friend Marguerite and I have started to learn rhythmic dancing under Madame Isodora in the hope that we might find our way to the stage."

An idea occurred to me and I proposed it to Rosina who accepted it immediately. We agreed that she and her friend Marguerite would come to my place at five o'clock bringing their dancing costumes with them. I gave her my address.

Forty-eight years have passed since that time in Paris, but they are the most beautiful memories I have—those sweet moments which fortune and the gods provide for us and allow us to experience.

That night I sat with Gibran on a comfortable seat sipping tea in a warm and dimly lit room. Olga sat at the piano in the faint light with a brocaded gray shawl falling about her shoulders, fluttering like a hundred butterflies in unison to the flowing melodies which her graceful fingers produced.

Rosina and Marguerite danced, their slender bodies, like the pillars of the Acropolis, swaying to the rhythm of the music. They danced wearing at first ancient Greek costumes, then changing to a flirtatious transparent wrap which endowed their animated beauty with a divine touch. Gibran and I watched in rapt adoration.

After the music and dancing party was over I tried to pay two francs each to Rosina and Marguerite. But Rosina, who spoke on behalf of the two of them, refused and said with all the dignity she could muster, "You are not Rodin."

"Unfortunately not," I agreed.

As she took leave she smiled joyfully and shaking my hand informed me, "I am free next week. I can sit for you Monday morning."

CHAPTER THIRTEEN

GIBRAN'S ILLNESS

☐ On the way to Madame Baudet's restaurant Gibran appeared pale and depressed. When I asked him the reason, he said, "Do you know, Yusuf, Rodin did not attend the afternoon party, and I do not feel well. My throat aches, maybe because I talked too much. I have no appetite. I have an appointment tomorrow with a movie producer, but I don't think I have the energy to talk with him in my present condition."

When we reached the restaurant Gibran bade me farewell, excusing himself, and continued to walk, supported by his cane which he always had with him.

As I entered the restaurant the first thing I saw was the face of my friend Calmie who was waiting for me. He was happy to see me and rose saying, "You are fortunate, my friend. I have succeeded in selling one of your paintings. Here, take five hundred francs. There is a demand for Cubism . . . If I were you I would hurry to paint another one and would make it as Cubistic as possible."

I was happy to receive the five hundred francs despite the fact that I hated this kind of art. It was for this reason that I heeded the advice of Calmie and spent all the following Sunday drawing confused lines, strange shapes and conflicting colors until I thought that I had achieved harmonious formation. Finished, I sat waiting for Calmie, reading *The History of the Origins of Christianity* by Renan.

While I was deeply immersed in reading about the Epistles of St. Paul, the coachman whom Gibran usually hired to do some errands came rushing to tell me that Gibran was sick. It was almost dark when I hurried to see Gibran, leaving word at the door for Calmie. He was lying on the divan fully dressed, his eyes closed because of the severity of the pain. Immediately, I lit the gas lamp. Gibran, sensing a movement in the room, opened his eyes with great effort and seeing me, he muttered chokingly, "Have you come, Yusuf? Please don't leave me alone. I am choking. I am going to die." In a weeping voice he moaned, "Mother, mother."

The maid rushed in while he was moaning thus, carrying a dish of warm soup. She said to me in anxiety, "Monsieur Gibran hasn't had anything to eat all day." In vain I tried to persuade Gibran it was necessary that he should sip at least a few spoonfuls of warm soup. But he insisted on eating nothing and turned his face away. He closed his mouth and continued to moan deliriously, which saddened me. My eyes filled with tears and I did not know what to do. I felt the agony of being a helpless stranger in a distant country.

At this moment I was rescued by the arrival of Calmie who seemed to me to have descended from heaven. When he knew what was happening, he told me rather brusquely, "I see that you don't know how to cope with such a situation, friend. Are you crying? That won't help. Call a doctor. I am going out immediately for a doctor."

He left hurriedly and returned after ten minutes, which seemed to me like a century, accompanied by a young man who quickly felt Gibran's pulse and examined his throat. He said with confidence, "Acute angina." He took several tablets from his bag and dissolved them in water, and began pushing the medicine down Gibran's throat with a small spoon. Then he gently pushed Gibran's head backward and moved the small spoon inside his mouth. Gibran quivered and began to cough and spit phlegm and blood which made me think that he had become better. The doctor advised me that it was necessary for Gibran to gargle once every hour.

After the doctor left I brought down blankets from

the attic and set them on the divan. I helped Gibran take off his clothes and put on pajamas. I stretched next to him on the carpet, reading *Le Pére Goriot* by Balzac. Then I dimmed the lamp and went to sleep. Whenever Gibran got up to gargle he said to me, "I am afraid you are cold, Yusuf. My overcoat is in the closet."

I answered him, "I am sleeping in my clothes, surrounded by angels. Cold can't bother me."

In the morning I lit the stove to boil water. I made tea and brought it with milk to Gibran. Gibran was exhausted, but he managed to drink a cup of tea and eat some biscuits and jam. He stayed in bed but he was not as quiet as he had been yesterday. He began to contemplate aloud the mystery of life and death, and, teasing, said, "What would you have done, Yusuf, if I had died yesterday?"

"I would have followed you," I said and added, "Now don't talk because talking will hurt your throat."

Gibran replied, ignoring me, "Your parents and sisters are still living. But my sister, my mother, and brother have died, and I don't know what has happened to my father." His voice choked. After a while he continued, saying, "I shall undoubtedly die before you, Yusuf. I beg of you now to place a statue of a roaring lion over my grave."

"And I beg you, Gibran," I replied, "to keep quiet—no death, no grave, and no lion."

There was a knock at the door. I welcomed Rosina and told her about Gibran's condition, apologizing that we were unable to work. I tried to pay her two and one-half francs, but she refused and said, "I have told you many times that you are not Rodin. Where is Monsieur Gibran?" She drew near him and like a compassionate mother she felt his forehead and turned to me anxiously asking, "Who is taking care of him and washing his clothes?"

"The maid," I said.

She shook her head in dissatisfaction and asked, "Where are the pillowcases, the shirts, the socks, and handkerchiefs?" She spontaneously got up and went to the closet, opened it, examined the clothes, and picked up what she thought needed to be washed without paying attention either to my or Gibran's objections. After she had changed the pillowcase, acting as if she were in charge of us, she wrapped the clothes in a bundle, placed it under her arm, and said while opening the door, "I will be back tomorrow."

Gibran turned to me with a questioning look on his sick face. "Do you think she will come back, Yusuf? She has taken the shirts and the socks. Do you trust her? Do you know her address at least?"

I said, "Take it easy, Gibran. I trust Rosina as I do my sister the nun, and I know her address here and in Italy." Then I told him about the five hundred francs, the price of the painting, and that I had an appointment with Calmie to deliver the second one to him.

Gibran then appeared to relax. He sat straight and said, "I am hungry, Yusuf. Bring me something to eat from Madame Baudet's restaurant—brains if possible."

In the evening Gibran felt better and insisted on taking a walk, promising to protect himself with a scarf. We walked slowly along the Seine, looking at and commenting upon the paintings and books that were exhibited there.

On the next morning Rosina returned with the bundle containing the shirts, socks, handkerchiefs, and the pillowcases, all of which were ironed, shining, and scented with laurel leaves.

We sat to finish the painting of "Carried on Angels' Arms". Gibran thought, as usual aloud, and began to analyze the nature of woman. He said, "I love women who are a combination of Beatrice and Messalina. But the great problem, Yusuf, is that when a woman is beautiful, her beauty in itself will be the cause of distrust. And if she were not beautiful or educated? Take, for example, this simple girl who is in front of us. She is a precious treasure, but what could we discuss with her a half-hour from now? In what conversation could we possibly participate?"

I turned toward Gibran and saw that the way the light

was reflecting on his face clearly revealed not only his features but his mental condition and that touch of melancholy which always hovered about him. I left Rosina and concentrated on him, and in less than three quarters of an hour his portrait was completed and I showed it to him. He looked at it for a long time and was pleased with it. Then he drew with his brush a circular frame around the chest, and asked if he might keep it. This portrait still survives among his belongings. It has been published in many books and periodicals.

While Rosina was dressing, Gibran opened a small box and took out a chain and three silver bracelets. He said to me, "I bought these things in Beirut and carried them with me to America and then Paris. Now I have found someone who deserves to have them. Give her this present, Yusuf, as if it were from you."

I told him, "How shameful! Do you want to teach me to lie, Gibran?" I then turned to Rosina and in her own tongue, said, "Accept this present from Gibran and thank him."

Rosina's eyes brightened with the jubilation of a child who has been surprised with a beloved gift. She could not control her joy and quickly replaced the string around her neck with the new chain. Nervously she slipped the bracelets on her wrist and then picked up Gibran's hand, attempting to kiss it.

I said to her, "Kiss him on the cheek."

She blushed, and Gibran blushed, too, and he let her kiss him without having the courage to return her kiss. He was bashful, and knew how to master love only in writing and words. During his stay in Paris, Gibran was not "Don Juan", as many have claimed.

CHAPTER FOURTEEN

WHAT IS LOVE?

☐ There is a popular tradition among poets which says that the gods sometimes become jealous of man's happiness and their jealousy drives them to act mischievously by molesting him. If these gods would act wisely and rightfully, they could make the path of man's happiness easier without losing anything, while increasing man's gratitude to them ten-fold. Their happiness too would be increased.

True happiness is to make those whom we love happy. How is this done? It is one of the great secrets of the gods.

In Italian one does not tell a woman, "I love you," but "I wish you well." This is how I felt toward Mademoiselle Olga. I wished her well and expressed my feeling by buying and arranging flowers around her piano and looking after them lest they wither. Sometimes, after returning home in the evening, I found a piece of candy on a small plate near the flower vase. One time I found a piece of paper on which was written the following: "If you are free tomorrow afternoon and would like to sit on the green lawn instead of shutting yourself up in the Art Academy, you will find me at three o'clock near the pear trees. These spring days are very beautiful."

After finishing my work at the Academy, I went as usual to the Dôme Café to spend the evening. At the first sight of Suzanne, I read in her eyes, those especially flirtatious eyes, that she had something to tell me and I sat with her. Calmie was among a circle of friends discussing the issues of the hour. Leah was listening between the two groups lest she miss some gossip.

Suzanne said, "Lend me your ears and attention. This time I have serious and important things to tell you."

I said to her, "You mean that the things which you have told me in the past were not serious and important —the philosophy of love, the trip to China?"

She said, "I am not joking this time. Please, you are different. You appear to those who do not know you as a man of considerable intelligence. Haven't you gotten on the fact yet that Olga is in love with you?"

Leah burst forth with her usual sarcastic laugh. I became more attentive and answered Suzanne with a mixture of joking and seriousness, "If I were, as you say, a man of some understanding, I should say, first of all, that I have a need to love, not to be loved. Love, Mademoiselle Suzanne, is an important matter. It is the most important and beautiful thing in life."

She said anxiously, "I pray you tell me then, what is your own opinion of love?"

I said, "First of all, I do not share your opinion that love is a drink of water and that woman is a dangerous plaything. I also do not believe that man is a means and the child an end, as Nietzsche claims in his book *Thus Spake Zarathustra*." Olga had given me this work to read and I had read it with mixed feelings of admiration and abhorrence.

Suzanne interjected, "Nietzsche was pessimistic because his love for Lou Salomé was unrequited."

Leah added, "Lou Salomé used to say that he had a grim look about him which suggested unhappiness. In other words, his looks were not like those of Gibran."

Suzanne interrupted her, "No doubt those who fail in love turn away from it to philosophy, philanthropy, reforming the world, or to composing poetry." Her eyes sparkled as she continued, "Be sure that I will not let you philosophize and compose poetry."

I said to her, "Believe me, if I did not philosophize, compose poetry, or reform the world, it would not be because of you!"

"To whom, then, would the credit go—to Rosina the Italian?" she asked.

"That is my secret," I said.

Suzanne, insisting, asked again, "Please, friend, at least tell me, what is love?"

I said, "It is not easy to answer that question in one word or a few words. Love is a mental attitude. It is a mystical experience akin to the artistic or religious feelings in which men lose themselves."

Leah laughed sarcastically and sneered, "Sheer words, a boring talk. I prefer a story about a priest or a Cappucine monk."

Suzanne silenced her by raising her hand and asked me again, "If it is not easy to answer my question in one word or a few words, I am willing to listen to a lecture on the subject provided that I finally understand your private opinion."

I said, "This would take us away from—as Calmie says —the practical subject. Have you been assigned by Mademoiselle Olga to carry out a mission? What does she want, exactly? We have lately sat for two hours on the green lawn discussing everything except this sentimental subject. Neither by words nor deeds did she do anything to show me that there is hot blood running through her veins or a heart palpitating in her chest."

Suzanne said, "You men are idiots and simpletons, especially you. Although Olga is older than we are, in matters of love she is still a child."

Leah heaved a long sigh as if to signify that she was bored by the whole thing. I said to her, deliberately changing the subject, "Draw near me in order that I may tell you a story about a Cappucine monk. It was ten o'clock in the morning on a very hot day; the monk was walking behind his donkey on a vast plain. He felt tired and tried to mount the donkey, but his feet failed him. He looked for a wall or a rock to help in mounting the donkey, but he could not find any. He could see no other alternative but to kneel on his knees and pray to St. Antonius. Then he got up and, putting his hands on the donkey's back, jumped with all his strength only to fall

127

down on the other side. He rose flicking the dirt off his robe and said, 'That was more than necessary, oh, St. Antonius, I did not ask for all that grace!' "

Leah smiled from ear to ear, and Suzanne drew near to me and whispered something which I shall not reveal now.

On the next day I received word from Sister Thérèse asking whether the paintings she had commissioned from me were ready. I answered that they were, and fixed a time for her to come and collect them. I readied the paintings of the Virgin: "Our Lady of Seven Sorrows" and "Christ in the Garden of Olives"; then I tidied up a bit for Sister Thérèse.

She arrived at the appointed time with the Mother Superior and another nun. They entered with immense dignity, the flaps of their white caps fluttering over their heads. They knelt in front of the pictures, crossed their hands, and said a short prayer. Then they got up, expressed their admiration for the paintings and thanked me. I asked them to sit down, which they did. The Mother Superior inquired about my health and affairs, and about news of my uncle the Patriarch, and my sisters, the nuns.

A wave of deep spiritual radiation and internal tranquility swept over me. The sight of piety and humility on the faces of these sisters was a revelation of true spiritual beauty. How distant I was at that moment from worldly affairs, the Dôme Café, the Art Academy, and the old streets of Paris—even the green lawn. All these things appeared to my inner being as cold matter compared with the pure and warm atmosphere created by the presence of these Virgins of St. Vincent. In vain, the devil within me tried to assert his mastery, but he was silenced by my deep inner faith.

Sister Thérèse had with her a small box wrapped with a blue ribbon which she presented to me. The Mother Superior said to me, "Truly we don't know how to reward you except by trying to express our sincere thanks and offer fervent prayers for your success." She invited me to attend mass on the next Sunday and to see the two paintings mounted at the altar. Then she rose and with the others took leave. Sister Thérèse carried one of the paintings and the second nun the other one. They left surrounded by a halo of holiness and purity.

I opened the velvet box and found an ivory rosary with a small silver crucifix attached to it. There was also a card saying, "Indulgence from the hand of the Holy Father," together with a dozen linen handkerchiefs having the first letter of my name embroidered on the hem of each. There was also a letter of thanks signed by the Mother Superior. I still have these objects as a beautiful remembrance.

Gibran listened to me relate my news about Olga, Suzanne, and the nuns of the Sisters of Charity, these subjects inspired him to eloquent flights of analysis finally ending in his suddenly asking me, "Do you love Mademoiselle Olga?"

I answered, "This is an intrusion into my very private affairs."

Then I confronted him with, "Have I ever asked you such a question? Truthfully, I don't know whether what I feel toward her is the love which you mean."

Gibran answered, "Love is love. It is a sweetness which runs through the blood. It is a sweetness, however, of so many innumerable varieties that almost every human being experiences a different kind of love. Love is determined by circumstance and fortune! Even perhaps by the height of a person or the color of the eyes. Man no longer lives in caves and jungles. His life and thought have evolved with time. The religious factor has had its influence upon us. The priests have enacted laws for love which I abhor, because they are motivated by ignorance, arrogance and injustice. The poor woman is forced to submit, and they laid out these laws and ordinances in matters of greater concern to her than to them. Then they ascribed their laws to the Creator while the Creator had nothing to do with them. If analyzed, these laws will be found far removed from the spirit of divine justice."

Gibran spoke with great enthusiasm and emotion, as if the subject had been occupying his mind for a long time. Then he returned to the original question, "Tell me, Yusuf, what do you feel toward Mademoiselle Olga?"

In order to satisfy him I answered, "I wish her all good and happines. I have built an altar for her in the depths of my heart and I have no intention of shaking or destroying it even if she wanted me to do so."

He said impetuously, becoming impatient with me, "And when did you begin to speak in a poetic language? If their feelings for each other were mutual and the lovers free, what is the objection to fulfilling their happiness?"

I interrupted, "Do I understand from what you are saying that you agree with Mademoiselle Suzanne that love is like a drink of water? No, Gibran! I cannot advocate a selfish and cheap sensual love. There is something within my heart which objects to it vehemently; it is stronger than reason and logic. Tell me, friend, where would love lead if we divested it of spiritual beauty?"

Gibran said laughingly, "Spiritual beauty? You talk like one of the Sisters of Charity. It seems to me that there are still within you traces of priestly influence."

Upon hearing Gibran's remark, blood rushed to my head and I felt almost insulted. This was the first time that we had had a heated argument. But instead of becoming furious, which was not my nature, I repeated the question, "Where would the love you refer to lead? Tell me, doesn't it end in something trifling and mean?"

He asked me sarcastically, "And where do you want love to lead?"

"To a lofty position," I replied, "which elevates man to the dignity of the gods and enables him to fathom the deepest and most wonderful mysteries, and urges him to undertake the greatest and noblest deeds."

Gibran said in a slightly less sarcastic tone, "Beautiful speech. I shall study this subject. It is worth studying."

I remarked, "You write it and I will put the writing into practice."

Thus the conversation ended between us without having turned into a really heated quarrel about Cupid, the god of love. We had not reached a mutual understanding, for in subjects of this nature, everyone has his own opinion.

CHAPTER FIFTEEN

WHAT DID OLGA WANT FROM ME?

□ As was my custom every morning I went to see Gibran. We sometimes worked and mulled over the problems of life; sometimes I let him repeat to me some of the things which preoccupied his mind and which he intended to write about. If it had occurred to me at that time to record everything that crossed Gibran's mind, it would have filled a thick volume. All of what he thought was interesting, but most of it was still in the formative stage. Many times he would say, "I have something I want to say but words do not obey me . . . Within me there is something formidable—I don't know whether it is a devil, or an angel, or a powerful spirit trying to . . ."

Before he finished talking I would interrupt him, saying, "How wonderful it would be, Gibran, if you tried to laugh. I am afraid that reading Nietzsche has too much affected you. I don't enjoy this stern philosopher who ended in madness. I like Leah's analysis of him. She says that his grim features suggest unhappiness in love. If he had laughed, probably Lou Salômé would have changed her opinion and would not have married someone else."

Gibran would say, "I see that you talk about love as if you were an authority, but only when the subject concerns someone else. When you yourself are the protagonist you feign ignorance. Suzanne has assured me that Olga is about to lose her mind while you have no pity on her."

133

I retorted, "Is this a conspiracy between you and Suzanne against me? If Mademoiselle Olga is about to lose her mind the question is simple. She should leave Paris. It pains me to see her neglect her studies. As for me, my friend, I assure you now and forever that I have no inclination to perform in a play, especially assuming the role of a protagonist."

Gibran said, "We always play the role of a protagonist whether we like it or not."

"Anyway," I said, "the waters of the Seine have long since receded to their normal level and the room of Mademoiselle Olga is no longer exposed to humidity or dampness. Therefore, it would be possible to take the piano back to its former place. You, Gibran, were the cause of Olga's moving to my apartment. Please make an effort to move her back to her place." I was serious.

After spending the evening at the Dôme Café I returned to my place to find that the piano was gone. On the table I found a four-page letter which I regret has not been preserved. For I now realize—after it is too late —how unique and precious that letter was. It was filled with philosophical, scientific and logical arguments in favor of the position that a woman has the right to have a child from the man who occupies her mind and heart. Olga also revealed that her father agreed with her on this point and that she did not have enough courage to speak to me openly about it. She was coming on the next day to receive an answer. She closed the letter with the following: "I pray you, my friend, if you cannot agree with my wish and if you insist on rejecting my request, to explain to me the reasons for your refusal, guided by your weighty judgment and great heart, lest I lose respect for you and for myself."

The letter hit me like a thunderbolt. A long night loomed before me in which to analyze the situation and look at it from every angle. I remember that for the first time in my life I could not sleep. My wakefulness compelled me to listen to the voice of my conscience. Shortly before dawn I reached a final decision, and that was to preserve the altar which I had erected for her within my heart. My soul was comforted by this decision. Although it was cruel, it appeared to me much more substantial than a temporary and fleeting sensual delight. Yes! I would act as she herself wanted me to in order not to let her lose her respect for herself and for me, and also I would not lose respect for myself.

On the next day Mademoiselle Olga came to see me with an engaging smile on her face—a smile which had lately disappeared. She knew when she first saw me that I had rejected her request. I explained to her that I was doing this to preserve her self-respect and protect her future. Then I told her that I wished to help her overcome this crisis and that I was ready to discuss the matter at length and support my words with action. But she turned and spoke to me quietly and with composure, saying, "Thank you, my friend, but my luggage is ready at the boarding house. I will leave Paris immediately . . . allow me, if you will, to kiss your forehead . . . a farewell kiss."

She kissed me tenderly and left. In bewilderment I stood at the window watching her get into a car and disappear at the curve of the street. It was then, that I fell on the couch holding my face in my hands and like a small child I broke uncontrollably into a severe fit of weeping.

Contrary to my custom I did not go to see Gibran that morning. After Olga left, I was immersed in a deep state of melancholy. I felt as if a strong hand were squeezing my heart.

Shortly before noon there was a knock at the door and it was Gibran. He had come to inquire as to the reason for my not having shown up at his place. He entered leaning on his cane and looked at me for a long time before he asked, "Why are your eyes so red, Yusuf?"

"I stayed up late last night translating Dante's *Divine Comedy*," I replied.

"That's not true," Gibran said. "When did you learn to lie? I have never known you not to speak the truth even if it cost you dearly." Before I answered him he put his hand in his pocket and took out a letter; I immediately knew from whom it had come. I noticed the handwriting of Olga on it. She must have written it after she had left me and gone to bid Gibran farewell.

Gibran sat beside me on the couch, and, as was his custom, he began throwing questions at me like an investigator working on an important case. He commented on my answers and analyzed the situation. He concluded, "I am proud of you, Yusuf. You have proved that you are honorable and that you have responded to your reason and not to your heart. It is not easy for reason to overcome the desires of the body."

"Ssh, ssh. . . ." I said, putting my finger on my lips. "Ssh, ssh . . . it is a private matter . . . very private. Its acts have ended in peace. Let us draw the curtain over it."

CHAPTER SIXTEEN

CALMIE'S MARRIAGE

☐ One day I encountered Suzanne alone at the bookshop dusting the books and paintings. She exclaimed, "You are mad! You have let Olga slip through your fingers. Why don't you teach your clever techniques to your friend Calmie? He is hooked; he is engaged and will marry soon. His story is not totally without humor. Come, sit down and I will tell you something about it!"

Not concealing my astonishment, I replied, "Is it possible? Is it true? My friend Calmie has been hooked? I thought he had more immunity and resistance to such a thing than me."

Suzanne shook her head and with a measure of defiance and a gloating tone, said, "You men think of yourselves as being immune to women. But each one of you will one day be hooked. Listen, and I will tell you how Calmie happened to be caught.

"We have a friend at the Office of Ceremonies in the British Embassy who invited Calmie to a ball for the occasion of the coronation of King Edward. Calmie jokingly asked his friend to introduce him to the guests as a 'Count'. Among the guests was a Miss Esther who had come from London to look after her father's business. She thought that she would like to be introduced as 'Lady' Esther. When 'Count' Calmie and 'Lady' Esther, who was as beautiful and charming as the 'Count' was handsome, met each other and danced, they fell for each other like a thunderbolt. Despite the fact that both the 'Count' and the 'Lady' discovered the other was fake, their love never faltered; indeed, it became stronger and stronger. Later on, they found out that they shared a common inclination toward business to which they decided to devote themselves after their marriage, which will be soon."

I listened attentively and somewhat amused to Mademoiselle Suzanne. But before I could say anything she vigorously continued, "For the occasion of Calmie's marriage we will hold a family party in our home. You are invited provided that you can persuade your friend Gibran to attend, or else Leah will die of grief. She is now busy helping my mother prepare some refreshments for the occasion.

"It is my intention to travel to China, you know, because we are thinking of establishing another shop in Paris similar to the one we have in London. This, at least, is what Esther would like. How wonderful it would be if you would listen to me and both of us could travel together. Believe me, art does not satisfy your hunger."

I replied, "And who told you, my friend, that my goal in life is to gather money? Gibran and I are preparing to leave shortly for Istanbul, Athens, and Rome."

She said, "Your motives are difficult to follow. I don't understand the benefit you expect to get from this trip unless it is to waste time."

When I told Gibran some of what Suzanne had mentioned concerning the invitation to the wedding he said, "The atmosphere would be Jewish in which I would not, as you know, be comfortable. I am afraid that we will feel like strangers. However, it is just an evening and Leah deserves some sacrifice from us. Furthermore, Madame Calmie does, after all, speak English. So, why don't we go? One thing remains, and that is a present. Is it appropriate to attend something like this with empty hands?"

I assured Gibran that our presence would be more than sufficient for a present.

At the party, ten of us sat at a rich table laden with all kinds of food. After eating, drinking, and dancing, Suzanne called for everybody to be silent. She said, "Ladies and gentlemen, we will close this party with a contest

138

which has a prize for the winner." She pointed to a red velvet box on a table near a candelabra which had seven candles mounted in it and said, "The prize will be awarded to the person who tells the most delightful story. I will draw three names in a row." In fact, there were only three names in the bag, or rather in Suzanne's hand, according to the instructions I had previously given to her.

Suzanne first drew the name of a young Romanian who told his story in Romanian and made those who understood it laugh. Then she drew the name of Leah who told a story about a Jew which made everyone laugh. Then she drew the last paper which contained Gibran's name. Everyone turned toward Gibran and clapped their hands to encourage him. Gibran became confused and looked at me with astonished eyes. I told him in Arabic, "It is now the turn of your courageous grandfather. Didn't he do anything heroic? You must have an entertaining story about him."

Madame Calmie insisted and urged Gibran in English to tell a story. When he found that he had no choice, he mustered all of his courage and began to relate a story about his grandfather whose name was also Gibran.

"It was my grandfather's custom not to leave the house without carrying his sword with him. He never even slept without placing the sword at his side. Once it happened that a bishop presented our town with pictures of 'The Way of the Cross'." Here, one of the guests interrupted Gibran asking about "The Way of the Cross". I came to his assistance and briefly explained the meaning. Gibran continued, "The priest hung the pictures in the church and tolled the bell calling the people to come and see them. My grandfather was among them, and, of course, he was carrying his sword with him. The priest began to explain, pointing to the first picture, 'Here is Our Lord Jesus Christ in the Garden of Olives . . . and here are the soldiers trying to arrest him.' My grandfather drew his sword halfway and his eyes flashed with anger. But he controlled himself and sheathed the sword to listen to the rest of the explanation. The priest continued, 'And this picture, my children, represents Our Lord Jesus Christ with the crown of thorns over His head . . . and this soldier is slapping him.' At this point my grandfather roared in a thunderous voice addressing the soldier, 'Here in Bsharri you dare slap Christ!' He drew his sword completely this time and struck out at the soldier, breaking the glass, the frame and the picture."

No sooner had Gibran finished his story than everyone broke into laughter and clapped their hands. Leah exclaimed, "The prize is for Gibran, the prize is for Gibran!"

Calmie commented, "Be thankful, my Jewish friends, that Gibran's grandfather was not living in the time of Christ. Otherwise he would have defended him and saved him from crucifixion."

Leah added saying, "And things would have been totally confused."

Gibran carried the velvet box, now all his, and we left shortly before midnight. The sky was clear with the bright stars spread across its vastness. A new moon peeked at us from behind the trees on both sides of the street. As we walked both of us looked upward with contented hearts. But soon, not being able to resist our curiosity we opened the box to see three pieces of Swiss chocolate and three other pieces of expensive coated candy. In the center of the box there were pictures of Suzanne and Leah contained in small frames. It was natural that Gibran gave me Suzanne's picture and kept Leah's for himself. He also gave me the chocolate and kept for himself the pieces of coated candy.

CHAPTER SEVENTEEN

MADEMOISELLE ALICE

☐ One day I met Leah alone at the bookshop. I noticed immediately signs of emotional disturbance on her face. She did not keep silent for long, and began talking to me, feeling comfortable in my presence. She said, "Monsieur Gibran passed by here and remained for a while looking at the paintings and reading through the books and periodicals."

I asked her jokingly, "Hasn't he inspected Leah's portrait and studied her features?"

She answered sadly, "No, not at all; he did not even pay attention to me. He was more formal than usual. In vain I tried to get him to tell me what was wrong. He said only that he had written some stories in Arabic and that they were sad morality tales. I asked him why he didn't write cheerful things and he answered only that fate has been cruel to him and that girls do not understand him. I did not understand exactly what he meant." After some thinking Leah asked me again, "You are his friend. Tell me, isn't there a woman in his life?"

I said, "We do not interfere in the private affairs of each other. Do you really care so much to know what there is in Gibran's heart?"

"Of course," she said.

At this moment before I could answer her question, a customer entered asking for a book. Leah went to attend to him and returned quickly, her eyes looking sadder and sadder. I put an end to our conversation by telling her, "I see that it is time to work at the Art Academy. See you this evening at the Dôme Café, my little one. We shall continue our conversation there."

Leah sighed and did not answer. I felt pity for this young girl who was so vulnerable to life and love. Oh! How many things are buried in the hearts of young women which men are too blind to see.

I was preoccupied with these bittersweet mysteries throughout the time I was drawing the model. There is nothing, while drawing a living model, more delicious than contemplating the secrets of the universe, approaching them sometimes with reason, at other times with sentiment, but without reaching a conclusion which satisfies logic or pacifies the heart.

The strangers who pay Paris a quick visit and engage in flirting with the Parisian beauties often come to the conclusion, in bragging about their amorous adventures, that by nature the French woman is an easy target. This is not true. I had the opportunity when I was in Paris to know many decent and honorable ladies, among whom were housewives and the saintly Sisters of Charity. In my opinion, people, be they black, white, yellow, or red, belong to one family. However, each has a different environment and adapts in such a way to circumstances and conditions that, one might say, every man develops his own kind of mentality and even physical appearance.

But this takes us away from our subject, which is the portrayal of the Parisian milieu during the short time that Gibran and I lived together there at the beginning of the twentieth century when we were in the full blossom of our youth. We had many friends and met many people who either did or did not affect the growth and formulation of our thinking and the development of our concepts of life and art. We were involved in these latter to the fullest while we were studying. Of all the cities of the world, Paris was the most generous in giving the things for which one searched.

One night while we were as usual gathered at the Dôme Café, Suzanne pointed out a young woman who passed in front of us, disappeared and then returned to pass once more in front of us as if she were looking for something. She turned to me and informed me quietly, "That is Mademoiselle Alice. She appears to be lost; indeed she is lost." Leah laughed scornfully, but Suzanne reproved her. "Don't be cruel, sister. Alice is a poor girl who deserves mercy and compassion. If I were sitting alone she would have come to talk with me."

The young woman passed in front of us for the third time. I looked closely at her face in order to understand Suzanne's remarks about her. I saw reflected on her pale and tired face the cruel and treacherous tragedy of life. I told Suzanne to call her to join us. She welcomed the idea and called her by her name. Alice did not hesitate and walked toward us attempting to conceal her nervousness. Suzanne calmed her down and made a place for her, assuring her that I was a trustworthy friend. She thanked us and threw herself on the chair seeking to rest her tired body and jittery nerves.

The waiter came rushing up with a towel in his hand asking for her order. I interrupted and told him, "Set the table for supper and bring me the menu."

Alice broadly smiled and said, "It appears to me, sir, that you are a prophet who can read people's minds."

"And predict what is in the stomach, too," I said laughingly. The clouds of worry on her bright forehead were beginning to be dispelled, especially after she drank the soup. She ate slowly while chatting with Suzanne while Leah and I engaged in small talk. After we finished eating, Mademoiselle Alice got up to leave. Suzanne wrote something on a small piece of paper and gave it to her, which she concealed in her bosom and Leah secretly put some money into her hand. Alice rose, thanking us and taking leave. She walked with firm steps and a raised head which bordered on the arrogant. I turned to Suzanne and gave her what sounded like an order: "Now tell me what's going on, and don't forget to tell me what you wrote on that paper, the meaning of the money, and where she is going."

She answered, "Leave her destination to the end; here is the story from the beginning. I have not known Alice for long. Two days ago when I was alone at the bookshop this young woman came in with a handsome young man and wanted to buy a book. I noticed that she examined the prices without regard for the subjects of the books. She chose a book for ten francs, which I wrapped and gave to her. Her companion paid for the book and both of them left. An hour later she returned alone with the book still wrapped. She was distraught with traces of tears in her eyes. I noticed that she was trying to control her quivering lips and it was difficult for her not to reveal her anxiety. When I saw her in this condition I gently took her hand and led her to the inside room of the bookshop. I made her sit on the sofa and tell me what was bothering her and asked how I could help her.

"After drying her tears she said, 'I am miserable . . . very miserable, and my story is sad. But you are a woman like me and no doubt you will understand what I will tell you. Perhaps you will be able to help me, for I am at the edge of the abyss.' After a deep sigh she continued, 'I came to Paris twenty days ago with fifty francs in my pocket.'

"'And why did you come to Paris?' I interrupted. 'Don't you have a family?'

"She answered, 'My father is a doctor in the town of ———— ————. I studied at a convent school and mastered handicrafts and typing. I came to Paris looking for a job, because life at home had become unbearable. My mother died a year ago and the maid took her place. I became a stranger in my own house and a burden to my father and his wife, or this is how I always felt. In order to get rid of me, my father and his wife tried to persuade and even force me to marry a young man whose social and educational standards were incompatible with mine, but he was rich. Is there greater misery than mine? Instead of throwing myself into the river, I escaped to Paris and rented a room for ten francs a month. I looked for a job in vain, while I spent all my money, and the end of the month was drawing near. This morning the concierge stopped me and told me that if I failed to pay the rent she would not give me the key. I had nothing in my pocket, not even the price of a cup of coffee. I went like a lost or

144

crazy person wandering the streets of Paris. At the entrance of the rue Vavin I met this young man who attempted to make my acquaintance and asked whether I needed anything. I answered him that I was in need of a book to read. And here is the book, still wrapped. So, if you want to help me, Mademoiselle, please return to me whatever you wish of its price. I swear to you that I am desperate.'

"This is Alice's story," Suzanne concluded, "and it is, as you see, not too much different from the story of those at whom the hypocritical Scribes and Pharisees used to throw stones or crassly insult. You have seen her with your own eyes; now let me tell you what I wrote on that small paper. It is your address. She is now going to sleep at her place, and tomorrow morning she is intending to visit you."

"Oh, great," I said. "Is this how you set a trap for me? I never expected you to do such a thing."

She answered, "Anyway, Alice is coming to see you tomorrow."

At this point Calmie came in with Dr. Casper and heard Suzanne's last words. Calmie pulled a chair up and sat, saying, "Is this, my dear, how you take care of women? I am afraid that kind of work at my bookshop will bring you more money than selling books."

"Hush," she said. "If your excellency were able, as you claim, to help her, why don't you then find a job for a poor girl who knows how to type?"

Concern appeared on Dr. Casper's face as he asked, "How is this girl's character and behavior? I am badly in need of a girl who can copy medical publications and reports. I would pay her well." Then he began to explain in detail the nature of microbes.

Leah drew close to me and whispered in my ear, "Let us allow them to talk about microbes, and I will tell you how Isaac won a great fortune which enabled him to build the largest store on the street of St. Germaine."

I said, "I am all ears, maybe I can benefit from the lesson."

She continued, "In one of the big German cities where

the hatred of Jews was intense, Isaac used to dress as a poor man, put on dark glasses, and sit at the entrance of the church with a placard in front of him. Written on it was, 'I don't accept charity from filthy Jews,' with the result that he was showered with marks from every direction. When his pockets became filled with money he went and emptied them into the bank of his friend Elihu."

On the next morning Mademoiselle Alice did indeed come to see me, carrying a big bouquet of white roses and wearing a most beautiful dress. I spoke, without inviting her to sit down, "Thank you very much—you shouldn't have bothered yourself. I love flowers, and you are undoubtedly a beautiful flower, Mademoiselle, but . . ."

After a period of silence I continued, speaking more seriously, "If you are really in need of work so that you might have food, shelter, and freedom, I have a friend, Dr. Casper, who needs somebody to copy medical publications and reports. Here is his address and his telephone number. You may call him by telephone from Bosohnet's store near here and make an appointment with him." Alice was arranging the roses in a vase without saying a word. Obviously, however, she wanted to say something. In order to prevent this, I said, "And if you don't like copying medical reports there is always shelter with the Sisters of Charity; ask for Sister Thérèse. Also my Art Academy would always welcome a model."

"Is that all?" she said.

"Yes, that's all," I answered.

"Thank you, Monsieur," she said, and departed the same way she had come, seeming not to care about anything.

CHAPTER EIGHTEEN

FATHER LOMTRE

☐ After dinner one night, we left Baudet's restaurant not knowing what to do. We were undecided as to whether or not to go to the Art Academy or rather, since it was a clear and warm night, to take an evening excursion during which we would give reign to our imaginations. But Gibran was tired. Thus, we stood at the crossroads, undecided whether or not to stay together or go our separate ways—I to the Dôme and Gibran to sleep—when I happened to look toward the café. I could not believe my eyes. There at the corner of the sidewalk our friend Dr. Casper and a priest sat around a table. Yes, he was a priest. His black garb left no doubt that he was a priest.

Gibran said, "Dr. Casper . . . with a priest . . . and at the Dôme Café? Has Mademoiselle Martine become reincarnated? I wonder what they are talking about."

Immediately we walked toward them, spurred by a spontaneous urge. When Casper saw us he unhesitatingly beckoned to us with his hands to join them. The young priest rose to greet us with an unassuming smile. Casper introduced us saying, "This is Monsieur Gibran and his friend from Lebanon, and this is my relative, Father Lomtre."

The Father stretched out his hand to greet us, saying, "I am very happy to meet two genuine Phoenicians." We said nothing. The Father, surprised at our silence, continued, "What! Am I wrong? Aren't you Lebanese Phoenicians?"

I said, "A very small percentage, perhaps, no more

147

than a drop of blood in the veins as a result of thousands of years of mixture, the last of whom were all Maronites."

We sat down. The waitress came back with coffee and cream. Dr. Casper further explained, "My cousin is interested in astronomy. He is studying a new theory about the origin of the universe. When he came to Paris he would not visit anyone until he had seen his cousin because, as you see, he was eager to talk with him. He is going to contact some archaeologists at the Louvre to inquire about the ancient Phoenicians, which relates to his interest. He and I are opposites regarding our scientific concerns. He is concerned with bigger objects, such as nebulae, and I with the smallest ones—microbes. But this great difference does not cause disagreement."

With this remark, Gibran looked as if he were holding the bull by its horns. He had not yet forgotten his heated argument with the Doctor about the existence of God, especially the Doctor's words about "you Easterners". Consequently he asked the Doctor, "Does not the belief in the existence or the nonexistence of God create disagreement between you two?"

The priest was not slow to comprehend the essence of Gibran's question. He smiled and answered, "Casper is of weak faith, perhaps with no faith at all. As for me, my faith is deep-rooted and is not subject to doubt. However, we are relatives and our relationship is amiable despite the wide gap between our principles and beliefs. My cousin has a kind heart and a sound mind."

Gibran agreed with him and said, "No question that kindness of hearts and soundness of minds are basic to understanding." He turned to me raising two fingers in an unconscious movement and said, "We are friends although we do not always share the same viewpoint."

While the conversation went on in this manner I wondered about the origin of the universe and the origin of all created things. I anxiously asked the priest, "Father, have you been able to understand clearly anything about the beginning of the universe except, of course, that it was created in six days or anything more than we know about Adam and Eve and the apple?"

The priest answered in a simple but serious manner while I listened attentively, "There is a possibility that the universe was at the beginning a conglomeration of substances. Your Phoenician ancestors claimed that an egg existed and one day was split as a result of some cause: the will of the creator . . . God."

I asked him jokingly, "Didn't God have anything else to entertain himself with, except hatching eggs?"

Upon hearing that, the priest smiled quietly to himself. At that moment Calmie arrived. No sooner had he greeted us and sat down than he became engaged in the conversation. When he heard from Father Lomtre about our ancestors' theory about the egg, he said, "These people baffle me; they invent many things but they do not know how to exploit their inventions or how to protect their rights. For example, they were the ones who taught the world the alphabet, but did not preserve their copyright. If they had charged those who have adopted and used their alphabet, by the beginning of the twentieth century they would have made billions."

I said to him teasingly, "Oh behalf of our countrymen, we entrust you with our case and, as usual, we pay you ten percent."

From this remark Father Lomtre understood that Calmie was Jewish, so he uttered courteous phrases about our fathers Abraham, Isaac, Jacob, and Moses, and about the Old and the New Testament, Christianity, and Islam. Also, he made reference to Buddhism to demonstrate his deep knowledge of religions. He joined Gibran in explaining and analyzing the externalities of religious practice and the reasons people have departed from the central points of religion, with the result that they have concentrated on superficialities rather than on what matters, and plunged themselves at times into the throes of a reprehensible and hateful fanaticism.

Of that conversation I remember a question which Gibran asked Father Lomtre: "Isn't it better for mankind in its present state of uncertainty to live as brothers on earth?"

The pious priest answered in the affirmative and added that all people need is a bit of magnanimity and tolerance. This, he claimed, was truly the meaning of religion. In connection with this he told us a story of an event which he witnessed. He began, "I was with Cardinal Marcet, the Archbishop of Malines, when a lady came to see him accompanied by her young daughter. She strongly complained to the Cardinal against the severity of religious and civil law. She mentioned that she was a widow and that her husband had served his country as a minister and an ambassador. She said that her daughter was presently engaged, but the Belgian law did not allow marriage without a baptismal certificate and that her daughter was not baptized because she and her husband had not placed importance on such 'childish matters'. Yes, this is how the lady spoke, and in the judgment of those present she was blaspheming. But the man of God reached out with a fatherly and Christian smile and asked the young woman gently, 'Daughter, do you want to be baptized in order to be married according to the laws?'

"She said, 'Yes, Father,' and lowered her eyes, blushing.

"The Cardinal said to me, 'Bring me a glass of water.'

"When I brought it to him he dipped the tip of his finger in it and signed the cross on the girl's forehead saying, 'I baptize you in the name of the Father, the Son, and the Holy Ghost.' Then he turned to me and said, 'Now give her a baptismal certificate in order that she might marry.' He turned to the girl and said, 'Congratulations in advance, Mademoiselle; I wish you happiness.' Then he asked the lady, 'Is there anything else I could do for you, Madame?' The woman thanked him with deep emotion and eyes filled with tears. She bowed down to kiss his hand which he hid out of humility."

The Doctor interrupted him, "Enough preaching; if you want to convert our friends, they are not in need of conversion. All of them are nice and their hearts are filled with love."

I turned to Gibran, commenting in Arabic, "The story

of the baptism is more beautiful than the story of the egg."

Gibran said, "It is closer to understanding and to the heart."

Gibran rose, bidding goodnight to the company. He was going to bed early since he could not endure staying up too late. I walked with him a few steps lest I miss his last comment on the subject. He said, "How wonderful it would be if there were a little kindness in the hearts of all religious dignitaries like the Archbishop of Malines. The action of the clerics under your uncle still echoes in my memory and occupies my mind."

I bid him goodbye saying, "I promise I will never tell about those goings on again."

CHAPTER NINETEEN

DR. CASPER
AND MONCADA

☐ "Are we not in this universe but a tiny atom, a germ which could hardly be seen sticking to a grain of dust lost at the entrance of a burning oven, in the light of a huge star which is one of forty million stars in one of billions of constellations?"

Dr. Casper surprised me with this question as I approached him at the Dôme Café. He was sitting alone burying his face in a scientific book which he was rapidly reading. As I sat next to him, pondering his question, he continued saying, "Man is a bone skeleton covered with flesh and fat, a tube for the digestion of food . . . he consists of billions of tiny cells."

I had no desire to listen to such talk or reply to it. In vain I tried to quiet him or change the subject, but it was like adding fuel to the fire, for the Doctor became more enthusiastic and talkative. He continued, "Man speaks by ejecting air through the mouth and moving the tongue in a particular manner. His speech might come out with or without meaning. For example: Se ma to yo si tan to. Do you understand the meaning?"

I sharply retorted, hoping to shame him, "Tell me, does Mademoiselle Martine understand everything that comes out of the mouth of the Doctor when he ejects a little air and chatters his teeth?"

He did not like my remark and shook his fist threateningly at me, "What have you to do with Mademoiselle Martine? I talk to her in the language which she understands."

I replied, imitating him by shaking my fist threateningly, "And she talks to you in a language which you don't want to understand. She wants to marry according to the laws in order to have a family and children."

At this point our conversation was interrupted by the arrival of some friends, among whom were Suzanne and Leah. I felt relieved and happy to see Leah wickedly smiling as she told me she had a story for me. But, instead, she asked me point-blank and with innocent sarcasm, "If He (God) existed everywhere how could He then move?"

I answered in the same manner, "He can always make miracles. Forget this nonsense and let us hear your story."

At another time, at the beginning of summer, I was as usual at the Dôme Café. Tables were set upon the spacious sidewalk and surrounded by chairs. The arrangement appealed to my friend Moncada, a middle-aged man of Italian-Spanish descent, who ran a small business in the Latin Quarter which brought him sufficient income to enable him to live comfortably with his French wife, who also was his business partner. Neither his small business, his wife nor his origin provoked my interest but his political acumen did. Moncada possessed extensive knowledge of many things about which I wanted to know. Furthermore, I found it delightful to talk with him in the beautiful language of Dante, especially since he was an admirer of the great poet. I remember how tears filled his eyes with joy when he learned that I was translating Dante's *Divine Comedy* into Arabic language.

The thing which drew most attention to my friend Moncada was his long beard. I would not be exaggerating if I said that his beard was the longest I had ever seen in my life. It reminded me of the beards of the venerable priests of Lebanon. How often I spied him in the evenings entering the Dôme Café carrying a bunch of newspapers under his arm. He would choose a table and clap his hands, calling to the waiter to bring him *Le Temps* and a cup of café au lait. Then he would become preoccupied with reading and stroking his beard from top to bottom. Every now and then he would steal glances at the passers-by and, of course, the ladies among them. When he saw me entering the café he always insisted that I join him.

Sometimes he said to me, "You, my friend 'Peppino', are a perfect man. I like all of your qualities. Without exaggeration you are the dearest of my friends here. But there is something in your behavior which I am unable to understand or explain. How can you find pleasure in the company of Jewish girls? How awful! Everytime I see you sitting with them laughing and exchanging jokes I become furious. Is it proper for you to behave like that when you are, as you appear to be, from a good family?"

I did not argue with him, but changed the subject. For instance I would ask him, "What do you think, my friend —will Italy occupy Tripoli and teach a lesson to the Sultan and to the men of the Committee of Union and Progress?"

He answered, "Yes, I think so. We are in need of colonies. Our country is getting so crowded we are about to swallow one another, while, at the same time, the sun never sets on the possessions of the English and the French."

The feeling of hatred was mutual between Moncada and the two young women. Whenever they saw me sitting with "the man with the ugly beard", they displayed their resentment in a thousand ways. Suzanne, for instance, would turn her face while passing by us, ignoring me as if I were a stranger. Leah, on the other hand, would grimace sarcastically and then stare blankly ahead. I could read clearly what was going on in their minds. How often I heard Suzanne say to me, "I do not understand, my friend, what pleasure you find in the company of that Italian. Is it befitting a man and an artist like you to lower himself to the extent of associating with such people?"

Leah would add, mockingly, "I could guess the days of the week by just looking at his beard and noticing the changes of its colors. It is like a calendar. On Sunday and Monday its color is pitch black. On Tuesday and Wednesday it becomes grayish with white hair appearing at the temples. On Thursday and Friday the white becomes dominant over the black. On Saturday it becomes black once more. I can assure you that it is the best calendar I have known. It cannot make a mistake."

Then Leah would release her resounding musical laughter—that sarcastic laughter which I loved to hear. I often wished Gibran were there to hear Leah's chatter and laughter. How many times she painfully whispered to me, "Gibran does not pay attention to me or care for me. What am I to do? He ignores me and is always busy with American women."

CHAPTER TWENTY

JULY FOURTEENTH

☐ It was the beginning of July. In a few days, that is, on the fourteenth, the national holiday of the French Republic would take place—the celebration of the destruction of the Bastille. Everywhere preparations were in full progress: triumphal arches, decorations, parades and fireworks. Also, there were all sorts of parties going on, not only in clubs and homes, but on the streets, sidewalks, and in public squares. At this time of year Paris becomes crowded with people from all over France and of every type. Every one of them forgets himself in the midst of the prevailing joy and has a time which is indeed memorable.

I said to Gibran, "Is it appropriate, Gibran, that we should remain in isolation without celebrating with the French? Don't forget that we are their guests and it is the least of the guests' duties to try to adapt himself to the people of his host country. What would be the objection if you and I should go in the evening of the holiday to the Dôme Café? It is not necessary to sit with anyone, but we can, if you wish, sit alone."

Raising his hand, his eyes sparkled, and with a delicate mysterious smile Gibran said, "Yusuf, the rope of lying is short. Mademoiselle Leah is undoubtedly behind this devilish plan. It seems to me that you do not speak except through her tongue. Yesterday I passed by the bookshop. She was alone like a bird in a cage. She suggested to me the same idea with a great deal of enthusiasm, hoping to persuade me. Strange is this young woman. Her speech belies her age. In my view, she is no more than a child.

However, her talk is sometimes startlingly profound, which makes me often wonder whether or not she repeats things like a parrot without really understanding what she is saying. Yes! She prevailed upon me to accept her invitation to the July Fourteenth party."

I said, "You mean to tell me that you have refused her invitation? How cruel your heart is, Gibran. Sometimes you seem to have no heart at all."

But instead of answering me, Gibran repeated to himself the following line of poetry:

"My heart is sore; who would lend me in its place
a heart without sores?"

I answered him in the same poetical manner:

"Three things drive grief away from the heart . . ." *

Then I added more seriously, "Tell me, Gibran, don't you find some similarity between the color of Leah's hair and that of Olga's? I know that you like blond hair . . . the very golden type." I went on joking with Gibran and talking to him in this manner until finally I succeeded in persuading him to attend the evening party on July fourteenth at the Dôme Café. How happy Leah was and how she clapped her hands and danced at the news! Sharing her great joy were Suzanne, Calmie, Doctor Casper, and Martine, all of whom in reality loved Gibran, were amused by his talk, and wished him all the best.

Gibran did not know how to dance. Perhaps he had never once danced in his life, and a July Fourteenth party without dancing was meaningless. However, I endeavored to persuade Gibran of the necessity to adapt to the situation. I reminded him that dancing, music, and love are among life's priceless blessings. It would be inappropriate if we were to appear ungrateful. I told him, "The procedure is simple, Gibran. Go up to Leah, po-

* These three things are: water, a green place and a beautiful woman.

litely bow before her, and ask her in as nice a way as possible, 'Mademoiselle, may I have this dance?' Naturally, she will gracefully rise and coyly accept your invitation. Stand facing her, holding her left hand with your right hand and put the other one around her waist. There is nothing more except to trot slowly, following the music like this: one foot forward, and the other backward."

After this so-called lesson I held Gibran's hand and led him, despite his laughing objections to the whole thing, through some practical dancing exercises. When I realized that he was amenable to further instruction, I said, "I will teach you how to dance without charge, provided that you do not disappoint me. I will break the glad news to Leah tonight that you will dance with her. I hope that you are taking this seriously."

On the next day I began to think about arranging some amusement which would be worthy of us. The first of the devilish ideas which occurred to me was to make two beards exactly the same as the beard of my friend Moncada. I sought Calmie's assistance to find two intelligent and witty young men to wear the beards and execute our plan. We kept the whole thing secret until the evening of July fourteenth.

At sunset Paris began to sparkle with festival lights. All of the people left their homes for the clubs and public squares. They laughed and shouted while dancing in collective or separate groups to the tunes of music which were being played here and there as if merry-making were the only concern of the citizens of Paris.

Soon, I began to worry as our friends had not yet come. Neither Suzanne nor Leah had arrived. There was no trace of Moncada, either, and without them our plan would fail. On my left Gibran began to yawn which sent fear into my heart that he might retreat. Therefore, I began inventing jokes to entertain him until the rest of the group arrived.

I told him, "In 1717 a young man, twenty-three years of age, named Arouet arrived in Paris. It was shortly after the death of Louis XIV. Since his successor, Louis XV, was still a child, the tasks of the monarchy were entrusted to his Regent. The king had nothing to do but indulge in his juvenile entertainments all day. For this reason anarchy began to prevail, forbidden things were permitted and moral corruption spread throughout the different sectors of society. This abnormal and excessively immoderate situation drew the attention of the proud and confident young man Arouet. He advised the dissolute Regent to economize by selling half of the horses which crowded the royal stables. Arouet further advised the Regent to dispose of all the 'asses' which filled the royal court. This brave advice soon circulated amongst the people of Paris. It was not long before they were ascribing to Arouet every caustic remark and biting joke. Furthermore, the people began to sing songs making fun of the Regent. Furious, the Regent believed that Arouet was the one who composed these songs. He had him thrown into the Bastille where he remained eleven months. It was during those months that he assumed the name 'Voltaire' and composed an epic praising King Henry IV which the Regent read with admiration. He released him and assigned him, as compensation, a salary. For this Voltaire wrote him a letter saying, 'Thank you for your concern to feed and clothe me. However, I beg you from now on to leave the problem of where to live up to me.'"

Gibran laughed and commented, "Voltaire is indeed delightful."

At this moment Moncada entered, accompanied by his wife, who hadn't counted in our plan. They were followed by Suzanne, Leah, and their mother along with Calmie. This also was not in our scheme. Fortunately enough, Moncada sat with his wife at a separate table reading his newspapers. Suzanne, Leah, their mother, and Calmie sat down, and the first act of the drama began.

Soon, a second Moncada entered from the right side and a third Moncada from the left side, and both sat beside the first Moncada imitating him in all his actions. Obviously, this attracted attention and provoked a great outburst of laughter. Everyone laughed except Gibran, who, being sensitive, had become aware of the seriousness of the situation. He whispered in my ear, "I am afraid, Yusuf, that something will go wrong."

All at once I had the same intuition as Gibran, and realized the gravity of the situation. I saw how my friend, the real Moncada, looked pale. His beard quivered with fury. He nervously searched his pockets for something. I rose to my feet and in a second I was near Moncada holding his arm and asking him in Italian to come with me. Like a robot he stood up, his eyes filled with anger.

He walked with me silently, looking at no one. When we were far from the group he muttered in a choked voice, "If only I knew who the rat was that concocted this mockery, I would wring his neck."

I answered with a heavy sense of guilt, "He must undoubtedly be a Jew."

He continued repeating his threats and furiously grinding his teeth, "Woe to him if he falls into my hands, I will tear him apart."

I almost choked. Moncada noticed my great anxiety and the good man thought that I was sympathizing with him, so he began to comfort me. When we were opposite the Lilas café, where the crowds were at the peak of excitement celebrating the holiday, we met some Italian friends of Moncada. I left him in their company and excused myself.

With heavy steps and lowered head I returned to the Dôme Café. Many factors were contesting within me, presided over by sorrow and regret. I repeated to myself, "This will be the last time. . . I shall not do this again as long as I live."

I was brought back to reality by the voice of Mademoiselle Martine who anxiously asked me, "What is wrong with you, friend? Are you ill? Do you feel pain?"

I turned to her and noticed that she was wiping her tears. I said, "And what is wrong with you, Mademoiselle Martine? Why are you sad and crying?"

She said, "I don't know what is wrong with me. The people are all celebrating by dancing and singing except the Doctor who does not dance or let me dance. He is there, sitting with your friend with the long black hair, talking about shameful matters. In vain I tried to close my ears and before exploding I escaped."

I said, "Come with me. The matter is simple. Undoubtedly there is a misunderstanding."

Through the boisterous and noisy crowds I saw Gibran listening to Dr. Casper who was talking with enthusiasm. I also noticed Leah sitting alone gloomily holding her head with her hand, as if she were at a funeral, while everyone was dancing—even her mother.

I approached them, but the Doctor did not pay me the least attention. Gibran barely glanced at me. I could hear only snatches of their conversation until finally, a question was addressed by the Doctor to Gibran: "Do you know, Monsieur Gibran, how animals breed?" Then the Doctor continued to tell things relating to this subject describing everything in detail, which once more disgusted Martine; she attempted to block her ears.

I could not help but raise my fist over the Doctor's head, threatening him, "Either you shut up or. . . !" Leah, who saw me threaten him looked at me with renewed interest and asked me to hit the Doctor in the head. Martine encouraged her, imploring me to quiet him. Gibran was afraid that I might listen to the two girls.

My friend Casper made as if he took my threat seriously and stood up, saying, "He who threatens to hit does not usually do so; I will teach you how to hit." He raised his fist to my face, but I held it tightly. At that moment, I noticed a police officer pass by with his colleague. He twisted his mustache and smiled to us, considering the whole affair laughable and childish.

When the scene between the Doctor and me was over, I winked to Gibran that it was time to act. He arose with exaggerated dignity and walked toward Leah who hastened to meet him and held out her hand. I in turn held Martine's hand and joined the dancers leaving the Doctor alone watching us from afar.

162

CHAPTER TWENTY-ONE

AL-RIHANI IN PARIS

☐ In the summer of 1910 Amin al-Rihani arrived in Paris from Lebanon. He stayed in the Commercial Quarter near the northern railway station and often came to see me at the Latin Quarter. Once, he found us busy drawing the "Carried on Angels' Arms". He began talking with Gibran, sometimes in Arabic and sometimes in English, while stealing glances at Rosina's naked body lying on the stand. Rosina noted him looking at her and jumped to gather her clothes and dressed in a hurry, muttering in Italian, "This man is not an artist. I feel shy in his presence."

In vain Gibran and I tried to persuade her that the visitor was our friend, a man of letters, and a burgeoning philosopher. She was not convinced and left after we agreed on a sitting at another date.

Gibran rented a horse and carriage and the three of us went driving through the city. We passed the Palais de Bourbon and the Parliament building. We only glanced at them, however, since we were not interested in domestic politics, looking at the universe from above as we did. We crossed the bridge over to La Concorde and the carriage began to climb Les Champs Elysees Boulevard, without exaggeration the most beautiful boulevard in the world.

Al-Rihani sat on the right, Gibran on the left, and I in the middle, which made Amin comment, "The Father, the Son, and the Holy Ghost," preserving for himself the title "the Father", for he was seven years our senior. Gibran was termed "the Holy Ghost", because he was like a spirit attempting to fly. I, to complete the trinity, became "the Son". Immediately "the Father" and "the Holy Ghost" began discussing both in Arabic and in English ways in which to reform the world. I interrupted their conversation saying, "Look there, brothers, how beautiful is the road to your right and the palaces. This is the Arch of Triumph. Long live the Emperor!"

Above the rattling of the carriage and from behind my shoulder Gibran said, "Our brother Yusuf is contented with the world as it is."

Amin nudged me affectionately and said, "This is my beloved Son. When the priests in Lebanon excommunicated me and my friends deserted me he came to the Froyka to visit with me and inquire about my affairs—this I appreciated."

We reached Les Bois de Boulogne. The carriage went on through it until the horse became tired and the cabman grumbled. Gibran paid him the fare and dismissed him.

We sat to eat our lunch in a quiet restaurant on the lake's shore as guests of al-Rihani. We did not forget that "a little wine gladdens the heart of man." Within earshot of the ducks which were swimming gracefully, al-Rihani and Gibran poured forth the cup of wrath on the exploiters of religion, indeed, on all religions generally, as Voltaire, Diderot and others had done one hundred and fifty years ago in perhaps the same place in Paris.

After forty-seven years I ask myself with sadness, "Where is Gibran and where is Amin? As Voltaire said, 'This universe is and will be forever.'"

In the evening we preferred to walk back on foot on the most beautiful of all the boulevards. Amin whispered in my ear, "What do you think of spending an evening at the Moulin Rouge?"

I answered, "I will go if you want to." But Gibran looked exhausted, so we accompanied him first to his place and then we went to Montmarte to see the most wonderful of all Paris night clubs.

On the way Amin asked me whether I frequented these cabarets. I told him that I had visited them only once out of curiosity and, a few other times, at the urging of friends, who were strangers to Paris.

He turned to me and asked, "And our friend Gibran, didn't he ask you to accompany him to these clubs?"

"No," I said. "We go to the theatre when we can afford tickets."

Amin and I sat among the others on comfortable seats in the front of the great hall. In front of us on the stage there was a flood of semi-naked women. They had braids decorated with jewels, painted lips, moving breasts . . . arms playing like snakes, sounds of singing and laughing. The music was very loud, and thick aromatic tobacco rose and filled the hall and fell to fill our noses, throats, and lungs, which made breathing difficult.

I turned to Amin and said, "This is a nightclub; are you happy, 'O Eternal Father'?"

Then the first act ended. The hall was filled with utter confusion. Men led the ladies to the bar where money was being spent recklessly, while al-Rihani and I sat like statues saying nothing and thinking nothing. We were strangers in that strange atmosphere. Suddenly I felt a hand patting my shoulder and saw the other patting Amin's shoulder. I heard a sweet voice saying, "Are you made of lead, gentlemen, or are you nailed to your seats?" Al-Rihani nervously shook his painracked shoulder and I scrutinized the face of the inquiring young woman. She said, "I am Marguerite, Rosina's friend, don't you recognize me?"

I said, "Who could recognize you under all that make-up and this dress which is really not a dress? What are you doing here?"

Maybe the way I spoke was intemperate, for Marguerite gave forth with an unnatural laugh and answered, "And what are you yourself doing here with this gentleman?" She stared at Amin's face, and Amin stared back.

I asked her, "Does Rosina come here, too?"

She said, "No, her brothers do not permit it. She has a jealous family, but I have no one who looks after me." She began to weep and laugh simultaneously and wipe her tears gently lest they remove her mascara and other

165

make-up. Finally she said, "I will not invite you to the bar for that will cost you a lot of money. This place, gentlemen, is a den of robbers."

However, Amin turned aside and took out of his pocket half a golden lira, which was a fortune in those days, and placed it in Marguerite's hand. I was surprised because I did not know what possesesd him to be so generous. There was nothing for the "beauty" to do but to hug Amin, kiss him on the forehead, and then disappear in the crowd, leaving between his eyebrows the stamp of her red lips.

"Wonderful, wonderful, Amin," I went on repeating, at the same time wiping the lipstick with my handkerchief.

Amin teased me gently, saying, "Don't wipe it off, Yusuf. It has cost me half a golden lira."

The signal for the second act was given but we had had enough of watching the flood of semi-naked bodies and inhaling smoke. Amin was restless and the pain in his arm had intensified. So we left and I accompanied Amin home. I rubbed his arm as his mother used to do at the Froyka. We arranged to meet at the Louvre on the next day.

CHAPTER TWENTY-TWO

WITH AL-RIHANI AT THE LOUVRE

☐ In 1910 it was seldom that a prominent Easterner passed through Paris. But if it happened that such a person did so and we met him, Gibran would ask me, "Have you found anything worth knowing about this 'important' person? Have you asked him if he has visited the Louvre?" The answer to this question would inevitably throw light on what we wanted to know about him and consequently we would classify every person according to his answer.

Here are a few examples of the answers I personally heard from people who held important positions in their country and the world.

"The Louvre. . . ? I think that I have visited it but I am not quite sure." (Liar)

"Yes, I have visited it just to say that I have done so, but I have not found anything in it except worthless antiques." (An ass)

"The Lou. . . vre? Yes, of course. . . I have spent in it a wonderful evening watching the dancing." (Lunatic)

"Of course I visited the Louvre and bought ties and handkerchiefs." (Naive—he believes that it is a department store.)

Thus end the answers which call for simultaneous laughter and sorrow.

"The Louvre," I explained to Amin as we visited it one day, "was once a palace of the kings of France. It has witnessed the greatness of Louis XIV. After the Revolution it was made into a museum. Look at its large windows overlooking the Seine and its rich gardens perfumed by flowers. See how the light penetrates through the windows to dance around the masterpieces and unique works of art. As Gibran says, 'We are in Paris.' In these numerous galleries are the evidences of the civilization of peoples and their masterpieces are exhibited with taste and care.

"Lend me your ears," I continued. "These are some of the artifacts of Egypt, Sumeria, Babylon, Assyria, Persia, Greece and Rome. And here are the masterpieces of the Renaissance. . . This is the statue of Zeus, the chief god, and this is the statue of the goddess of victory, and this is the Mona Lisa—La Gioconda."

Thus we kept moving from one gallery to another and from one wing to the other for three whole hours. I did not feel tired nor did Amin become bored listening to me.

It is the custom of those who have not experienced art or who have no deep understanding of it not to be able to distinguish between the subject and the eloquent or poor expression of it. They fail to understand it thoroughly. If a portrait or a statue, for example, were of a beautiful woman, they immediately would judge it as being of utmost artistic excellence whether it revealed perfect craftsmanship or not. I mean that the basis of their criticism and/or appreciation is not based on applicable rules and principles.

This was the attitude of Amin al-Rihani when we visited the Louvre together in the summer of 1910. He did, however, ask questions and endeavored to understand the true worth of the masterpieces he observed. Sometimes he commented on them with a philosophical insight which was not without merit. For instance, he told me, as we stood looking at the Assyrian statues, "The person who thoroughly scrutinizes these statues cannot help but see their cruelty."

"And what about the Egyptian statues?" I once asked him, to see what he would answer.

He said, "They have a touch of holiness and humility.

168

This Pharaoh, who is standing with one foot forward and the other backward, and those who are sitting with their hands on their knees appear to me as 'good people', closer to being gods and dignitaries."

"And these Greek statues. What do they reveal to you, Amin?", I asked.

He said, "Beauty, poetry, and love."

"Well done," I said. "You have understood their story easily. I shall hand you a 'diploma'. . . And the lady standing there?"

He said, "She looks as if she were from our country." He drew close to the statue and read on its pedestal, "The Empress Julia Domna, c. 200 A.D."

I said, "You are not mistaken, Amin. This Julia is a native of our country. She first saw light under the sky of Syria in the city of Hims on the Orontes River. She married the Roman commander of the eastern armies, Septimius Severus. With her beauty, intelligence and money she pushed him to the Imperial throne. With him she occupied the Palatine, the Caesars' Palace in Rome. There, she gathered around herself men of letters, scientists, and philosophers, and astonished the men and women of Rome."

Amin was moved by what I said and, shaking the pain from his arm, he said, "I feel sorry for her standing now on a pedestal in this cold hall on the Seine and being in this strange land instead of standing in a square in Hims."

"Are there squares in Hims, and who has heard of the name of Julia in Hims?" I asked. "On these black stones are inscribed the laws of Hammurabi, the origin of all laws—even the laws of Moses, and here, on the Egyptian-like tomb of King Ashmunadhar of Sidon is inscribed the longest example of Phoenician writing. The inscription beside this stone over here, in the corner, states that this is the slab stone of the tomb of Imru' al-Qays, the King of the Arabs."

In vain we tried to read the inscription engraved on the stone. As we gave up, Amin began reciting with emotion and grief, "Oh, neighbor, we are both strangers here."

When al-Rihani's visit to Paris was over, Gibran accompanied him to London where they remained for a whole month. They wrote me a letter which revealed a cheerful mental state. They were still at the beginning of the road and had not yet been completely bowed by the burdens of philosophical awareness and the disturbing fleetness of life.

The letter was not more than ten lines. Gibran began the first line and Amin the second, and so on until the end of the letter. Its content was gay and I was delighted by it. Soon, however, al-Rihani had to continue his journey to New York, and Gibran returned to Paris.

Thirty years later, in the Spring of 1940, my friend Amin and I were sitting on the porch of his home in Froyka, Lebanon. In front of us stretched a huge valley while to our right rose the encircling mountains crowned by the snowy white crest of Mt. Sannin. Amin was smoking his pipe and remembering his past, something which he seldom did. He mentioned his journeys to the Arab countries. He talked about King Hussain, the Imam Yahya, Ibn Sa'ud and Faisal as well as the future of the Arabs. Amin loved the Arab people and wanted to see them thrive, but in this discussion he was pessimistic. Finally, he ended up by mentioning certain individuals in Lebanon. In reference to these latter, his judgment was harsh and critical—harsher than I had ever known it.

"Be sure," I replied in turn, "that this universe will remain as it is and that you and your criticism will never reform it very much. We should be concerned only with our own affairs."

He answered me, still unconvinced, "It is still early, Yusuf."

We talked about Gibran, and how he had gained a certain amount of financial success from his writing and his art. I said, "Gibran knew how to calculate perfectly."

He answered, opposing, "No, he made out in the end because he was successful in choosing subjects which have salability and in becoming acquainted with publishers."

I asked him to explain to me the subjects which concern the Anglo-Saxon reader. He said, "Public opinion is in a chaotic state, especially since the advent of the cinema and the mass popularity of detective, semi-historical, and second-rate philosophical works, and adventure stories. There is a demand for all of these subjects. But what counts in the first place is the publicity put out by publishers . . . and luck, too, has its role."

Then we resumed talking about the past, including his visit to Paris, the excursion to Les Bois du Boulogne, the evening at the Moulin Rouge, and the visit to the Louvre. Finally Amin said, "That visit, Yusuf, was the starting point of my understanding of art. After it the horizon of my knowledge broadened and after much studying I turned to writing about the arts. I even married an artist. Whenever I had an emotional crisis I remembered that beautiful Parisian at the Moulin Rouge to whom I gave a gold piece as well as that girl at Gibran's studio who resented my staring at her while she was naked . . . I remember that, Yusuf."

I answered him instantly, "I, too, remember that and will not forget it."

That summer, my friend Amin al-Rihani died at Froyka. He now rests at his family's mausoleum under the shadow of two embracing oak trees. I visit him once a year to contemplate the destiny of man and shed a tear.

CHAPTER TWENTY-THREE

ISADORA DUNCAN'S VISIT

☐ After al-Rihani had departed for New York, Gibran returned to Paris. We resumed our former pattern of existence—painting, discussing art and life, taking walks along the Seine. Whenever invited, we went to the Théatre du Chatelet to watch the famous American dancer, Isadora Duncan. Sometimes we had a little party at my place during which Olga played and Marguerite and Rosina danced. There, in the faint candle light Gibran and I watched, drank tea, and dreamed.

At that time Gibran was preoccupied with writing. Sometimes he read to me what he had written. As for me, I was under the influence of Renan due to having read his seven volumes of *The History of the Origins of Christianity*. Into these volumes Renan had poured all of his vast knowledge, presenting the subject with such skill that my admiration was unbounded. I told Gibran, "How wonderful it is, brother, to specialize in one art or science. The role of prophet does not appeal to me. Nor do I care to indulge in nebulous abstractions. I could not care less about reforming the universe. I care only about understanding something clear about the mysteries which surround us."

Gibran answered in something like sarcasm while sipping coffee and puffing on a cigarette, "Tell me, Yusuf, in what kind of art or science would you like to specialize? Do you think that it is in your power to understand one single thing clearly about the secrets of this colossal, astonishing universe?"

One day I asked him his opinion about the statue of a dancer on which I was working. He looked at the statue for a long time and examined it with the eye of an experienced and meticulous artist. He said, "Congratulations, Yusuf! No doubt your dancer is inspired by Isadora. You are definitely a better sculptor than a painter. Specialize in it."

He spoke as he prodded the clay, touching some of the body's lines with his finger, while I teased him in my special manner, "You are going to dirty your finger . . . and the beautiful ring on it."

He asked to see the original painting from which the statue was copied. I told him that Marguerite liked the painting and I had given it to her as a gift. Gibran got mad at me and said furiously, "You are too careless with your paintings. You need a guardian!"

I answered calmly, "Patience, brother. It seems that Isadora saw the painting at Marguerite's and liked it. She inquired about the artist and she might visit me."

Gibran shrugged his shoulders scornfully and said, "Sheer fantasy, Yusuf! She does not even condescend to visit the richest of her fellow Americans, the millionaires."

However, after some thought, Gibran mused aloud, "Who knows? She might appreciate and understand art. Anyway, she is rich, and she probably despises her rich countrymen because they are ignorant. It is said about her in American society that she is arrogant. Men of letters and even poets humble themselves at her feet."

I said, "The only thing about her that I am really intrested in is her wonderful rhythmic dancing that has opened my eyes to new and vast horizons of art. Before I saw her dance and express the feelings of the heart and soul, I believed that dancing was a useless and childish twisting of the body."

Gibran interrupted me, speaking, as was his habit, like a prophet. "It is not the splendid dancing which opened before you these horizons, it is the atmosphere of Paris where the fingers of the gods move. Oh! How happy we are here. How far we are from the world of selling and buying, the gloomy world of theology, and the world of degenerate politics. No, Yusuf! The gods have offered us precious treasures which we have to protect from the thieves of darkness."

On the morning of the next day I received the following letter:

Dear Sir,
If you permit me, I and a friend would like to visit you next Thursday morning at eleven in order to become acquainted with you and your art.
Thanking you in advance, please accept, Dear Master, my regards and greetings.

Isadora Duncan

At the appointed time the famous dancer came with a companion. I received her in my working clothes. She asked, "The Master?"

"Yes, Madame," I said.

Her eyes expressed surprise. She walked toward me gracefully, stretching out her soft hand. "I am Isadora Duncan and this is my friend, Miss Johannsen from Copenhagen."

The dancer's eyes wandered around the room and she said as if talking to herself, "Exactly how I expected it to be—simplicity, paintings, books, and flowers." Then looking at me she spoke with her friend in a language which I did not understand. She continued in French, directing her speech to me now. "First of all, where is Lebanon? Do you have a map?"

Immediately I spread before her a small map of Asia and indicated with a red pen the eastern part of the Mediterranean Sea. She put on her glasses and began to read in a loud voice, "Damascus, Jerusalem, Lebanon. But where is Lebanon? D'Annuzio has told me that Lebanon is the country of Adonis and that it is covered with cedar forests."

I said to her, "The mountains of Lebanon, Madame,

175

were like that in ancient times, in Adonis' time. Today nothing is left of the thick cedar forests except a small holy 'oasis' on the mountain tops."

Miss Johannsen laughed and commented demurely, "And I stupidly imagined that Lebanon was a high mountain with a cedar tree on its top." With eyes as blue as the sky she gave me a long look filled with a vague but sweet meaning.

The prominent visitor contemplated the statue of the dancer while I was noticing the few gray hairs which had invaded her temples and the purple hue which engulfed her eyes. She asked me, "Tell me, have you seen Isadora dancing more than one time?"

"Many times," I said.

She added, still contemplating the statue and without looking at me, "Do you know her out of costume and do you love her always?" Without waiting for the answer she continued, "Please show me what paintings you have. I have seen one of your paintings which I greatly admired and desire to see more."

She began looking through the collection of paintings I placed before her. She chose two paintings and Miss Johannsen chose one. Isadora asked, "Can you spare these paintings?" And then, "Your autograph, please."

Each one of them took out a check book and a fountain pen from her handbag and wrote some figures. Finally Isadora said, "Allow us to offer you a small present. This is not the price . . . art is priceless, Master." Gently she left the two checks on the desk and said in a humble voice like a whispered prayer, "A small present and a souvenir from Isadora—a token of affection and appreciation."

She gave me her hand, smiling gracefully. I kissed it with great respect and accompanied her to the door. Before the car left, Isadora, smiling, raised her fingers to her mouth, throwing me a kiss from afar, as did Miss Johannsen.

I returned to my studio sadly, feeling a vague and disquieting emptiness, but soon I remembered the two checks. They were for a hundred dollars each and the dollar was at that time equivalent to five francs, twenty centimes. I remember that very well because Gibran and I spent some time doing calculations, subtracting, multiplying, and dividing.

CHAPTER TWENTY-FOUR

GIBRAN'S DEPARTURE

☐ I added the two hundred dollars to what money I had saved for my intended trip in August. I visited some cities in Germany and Austria. When I reached Istanbul I found a letter from Gibran waiting for me, the contents of which were the following:

You are, of course, happy in the city of the emperors and sultans which stands like a question mark between East and West. But no matter what, you will return from this grove of happiness haunted by the shadows of past generations and the fantasies of the present.

There are many things in Istanbul which require study and contemplation, particularly ancient churches and mosques adorned with Byzantine engravings and pictures which precede the Italian Renaissance. Make sure that you do not leave Istanbul without studying them thoroughly. The Imperial Museum contains many precious Greek and Roman objects. Look at them and remember me when you stand before an object of magnificent beauty and beautiful magnificence.

How did you find the Syrians in Istanbul? Are they living and active or are they stagnant and dead? The Syrian, Yusuf, is a sheep in his country and a lion in a strange land. If this is true of the Syrians of Istanbul, then announce the good news of this great success to Syria.

Here I shall pass rapidly without describing anything I saw of the masterpieces in Istanbul or elsewhere. However, I was constantly in contact with Gibran, conveying to him throughout our correspondence the most important of my impressions about art which space does not allow me to mention here. I continued my travels to Athens and Rome, and I returned to Paris via Florence and Geneva. I found Gibran busy preparing some paintings for the Fall Exhibition. He was obviously worried and disturbed because his financial situation might force him to return to Boston. Therefore, before this could happen, he wanted to make sure of participating in the Fall Exhibition.

Of his paintings, Gibran presented his "Carried on Angels' Arms" and two others; only one of the three was accepted. However, it was destined to be placed in one of the secondary corridors rather than in the big gallery as he had hoped. In the evening, Gibran revealed to me that he was very worried. He said, "Rodin, Yusuf, must be visiting the exhibition. How I would like to show him some of my work and hear a word of appreciation from him which would have an echo in American society! As you know, he does not attend exhibitions unless surrounded by some American ladies. It is not right that my painting should be exhibited in the corridor! How can they do this to me?"

Gibran stood up and began to nervously pace the room. I said to him, "Take it easy, Gibran. The solution is simpler than you imagine. Let us bribe the guard and I guarantee that he will move the painting to the gallery." It actually happened.

On the first day of the exhibition, I was standing on the other side of the gallery when Rodin entered, looking like a demigod. He was surrounded by a covey of perfumed ladies wearing long, wide dresses, high heels, and big hats sprinkled with colored flowers. I saw Rodin stop for a moment in front of Gibran's painting. Gibran walked a step toward him, stretching out his hand to greet him. He spoke a few words which I could not catch, and I never asked him what had been said. Rodin nodded his head to the fledgling artist and moved on to continue his round, accompanied by his flock of scented ladies.

Thus finally did Gibran meet Rodin, who was at that time over seventy and at the peak of his fame. He had produced many masterpieces: "The Age of Bronze", "The Citizens of Calais", "The Kiss", "The Thinker", "Hugo", "Balzac" and others. He was surrounded by a halo of fame, wealth and arrogance. Gibran was a young man—twenty-seven years old—and a stranger in Paris. He spoke French with difficulty and was trying, with toil and poverty, to make his way. As for his works and writings at that time, they did not provide him with income nor did they attract attention. Everything that has been said about his relationship and apprenticeship with the famous sculptor, the certificate of honor which he received from the French Art Academy, and his honorary membership in the English Painters' Society is nothing but falsehood.

The modern art movement had reached maturity in Paris at the beginning of the twentieth century. However, Gibran was neither influenced by nor did he pay much attention to it. His head was filled with all sorts of philosophical, didactic and symbolic concepts as well as many obscure things which he himself had not yet fathomed or concretized. The man of letters in him dominated the artist. Between his fingers, art fumbled its way with effort to establish its identity. Therefore, the artistic benefits which he obtained from his stay in Paris were not of great importance. He was forced to leave France, which he loved, at the end of the fall.

I accompanied him alone to the Lyons railway station, helped him to find a comfortable seat beside the window, and put his luggage on the net above the seat. I sat beside him and we spent the remaining few minutes with talk and final instructions. When the signal was given for the train to move, I got off quickly leaving Gibran to occupy two seats alone and stretch his legs comfortably. Nothing teaches a man and opens his eyes to the world like traveling.

Gibran continued to correspond with me. Every now and then I received letters from him expressing his nostalgia for Paris. One of these is the following:

Boston
January 19, 1911

Brother Yusuf,

Happy is he who has a place to lie down in Paris, and happy is he who walks along the banks of the Seine browsing through the stands of old books and admiring the paintings.

I am in this city, which is full of friends and acquaintances, like someone banished to the end of the world where life is cold as snow, gray as ashes, and silent like the Sphinx. My sister is near me and beloved ones are everywhere around me. People come to my home morning and evening, but I am not pleased with my life. My labors are approaching the mountain's top. My mental state is calm and my body enjoys good health. However, I am not happy, Yusuf. My soul is hungry and thirsty for food and water and I do not know where they are. The soul is a heavenly flower and cannot live in the shade, but thorns thrive everywhere. Al-Rihani is living near New York. His life is miserable. Each of us complains to the other about the sorrow in his heart and each of us longs for Lebanon and its beauty. Such is the fate of the sons of the East who are stricken by the disease called art. Such is the life of the sons of Apollo who are exiled to this world with its strange deeds, slow pace, and laughing tears. How are you, Yusuf? Are you happy among the human shadows which you see on both sides of the road? How is your work coming? Are you satisfied with it? And what have you painted in my absence? Mrs. Hamilton wrote good things about you to me. Remain her friend, for she is nice. Moreover, she is one of the martyrs of the tyrannical yet compassionate, dark yet bright god of art. How far have you gotten in translating Dante? Are you in his company in that bottomless abyss among those dangerous crossroads? And to what point have you been led by "She with the golden hair, the companion of Botticelli's soul?" Are you standing by her in the face of eternity among those strata which are far removed from the world of measure and quantity? I have many ideas which struggle between the depths of hell and the heights of heaven. But I do not want to submit them to ink and paper. Remember my name at the Louvre and in front of the Goddess of Victory. Greetings to the Mona Lisa. Greetings to the hovering spirits over your head. Greetings to you from your affectionate brother,

Gibran

CHAPTER TWENTY-FIVE

ROSINA'S DEPARTURE

☐ About one A.M. I was in bed reading as usual when I heard a knock at the door, or rather, three knocks followed by three more. This was the knock of Mademoiselle Rosina. I wondered if it could possibly be she at this hour.

I jumped out of bed, stumbling, and descended the stairs to the door. I opened it and was face to face with Rosina. She was as pale as a wax statue and trembling all over. Sorrow and exhaustion were revealed in her face. She entered and threw herself on the divan, covered her face with her hands, and broke into a storm of tears.

I let her cry while I went to light the gas stove to prepare a cup of coffee—which was the best thing to calm her nerves. After a few moments, while she was sipping her coffee slowly, staring, and not saying anything, I said, "Come on, tell me what's happened."

She answered in a choked voice, still trembling and biting her lip in order to constrain her tears, "They kicked me out, beat me, and threatened to kill me. If it were not for the knowledge that I could find a safe refuge with you, Monsieur, I would have been by now at the bottom of the Seine. Oh! How I wish I had not come to Paris!"

She resumed crying and wiping her tears and I kept trying to soothe her. She told me that at first her brothers prevented her from going out at night. Now they had begun drinking and had asked her to do something even harder. They wanted her to become a prostitute. She implored me, saying, "I beg you, Monsieur, have mercy on me and help me return to my country. I have no one but you. May God reward you." She bowed down to kiss my hand but I hid it before she could kiss it.

Seeing her in this state, I assured her, saying, "Don't worry, my dear. Forty-eight hours from now you will be with your family in Anticoli."

She exclaimed, laughing and weeping at the same time, "Is it true what you say, Monsieur? I was not mistaken when I resorted to you in my trouble?"

I said, "You had better get some rest; you have a long way to travel tomorrow. I will give you my blanket. Sleep deeply and soundly. And if you are hungry there are biscuits and jam on the table."

I went up to the attic where my bed was and threw the blanket to Rosina—the only cover I had. She quickly pulled the blanket over her head for she really was overcome from cold and exhaustion. I rummaged for whatever clothes and woolen things I had and piled them over me.

I tried to read but could not concentrate, so I turned off the light. Sweet recollections swarmed through my head; Gibran and I had often discussed the nature of relationships between man and woman.

I finally drifted off to sleep and woke in the early morning. I descended slowly and lit the gas stove to make coffee. Rosina was still sleeping like a child. A lock of that golden hair which Gibran had so loved protruded from under the cover as if it were saying, "Yes, I am Rosina herself, the companion of Botticelli's soul."

Finally she awoke and removed the cover from her head. When she saw me, busy making coffee, she said good morning with a bright smile and began straightening her beautiful long and flowing hair.

I took her a cup of coffee, caressed her head with my hand, and kissed her forehead hoping that she felt better than yesterday. She innocently returned my kiss and said, "I do, indeed. When is the departure, Monsieur? I have dreamed of Tivoli's mountains and Anticoli."

"The train to Rome leaves at ten. You still have three more hours. Do you need anything else?" I inquired.

She closed her eyes and touched her forehead as if to collect her thoughts. Then she quietly slipped the three silver bracelets off her hand and asked, "Is it possible to sell these? I am in need of a warm dress and shoes. My present shoes are torn and water gets into them. My dress is light and I am afraid of catching cold going across the Alps. Moreover, I feel ashamed to go home with this patched dress and these worn-out shoes."

"Rosina, please return the bracelets to your wrist," I said, "and don't forget that they are a present from our friend Gibran. Don't worry. We will buy all that you need on our way to the station. I am going now to buy something for breakfast."

She shyly asked me to give her a needle and thread before I left.

I went to a nearby restaurant and found its owner, my friend Bochnet, in his white apron arranging cups of yogurt in the window. He smiled when he saw me and said, "Thanks to your having taught me how to make yogurt, my customers find Bochnet's yogurt better than that of the Bulgarians" (who monopolized yogurt at that time). "What can I do for you?"

"I need something for breakfast and provisions for traveling, and two hundred francs, which I will return to you this evening if I can or else next week."

The good man answered, "Monsieur Joseph! Everything in this store and its owner, too, are at your disposal."

Rosina spent some time fixing her clothes—the green dress, the white sleeveless shirt, the red shawl. These were all the clothes this poor young girl possessed to cover her body, the most beautiful of all bodies.

I sat in the same spot where Gibran and I had many times sat, listening to the music and watching the girls dancing. My mind wandered, and I thought, "Mademoiselle Olga is now in Tomsk saying, 'When I think of Paris it appears like a far-away dream.' Gibran is in Boston yelling, 'I am not pleased with my life, Yusuf!' "

As if Rosina were engaged in the same thoughts as I, she asked me, "Have you heard from Monsieur Gibran?"

"Yes, he always asks about you," I said.

She said, "When you write to him, please give him my regards and tell him . . ."

"Tell him what?" I asked.

She said, "Tell him that whenever Rosina looks at the silver bracelets she remembers him with gratitude and that she almost sold them to buy shoes."

She coyly glanced at me while saying this, knowing that I would never do such a thing. I instantly asked her, "Rosina! Tell me the truth. What do you think of our friend Gibran? I know that you sat for him during my trips and that he sometimes invited you to eat with him."

She said, "Gibran, Monsieur, is a prince, kind and refined. He has never done anything inappropriate. I did not always understand what he said, since his speech was above the level of ordinary speech, but it was enjoyable and interesting."

She thought for a while and then continued, "Once I almost got angry with Marguerite because she told me that Gibran was like all other men. One day he had invited her to lunch and told her that he loved two women: Beatrice and Messalina."

At this point I could not keep myself from laughing and said to her, "Gibran could not express himself in French. Beatrice and Messalina are nothing but symbols."

She said, "Yes, I told Marguerite that they don't eat and drink like we do. She did not believe me and replied, putting the tip of her finger on her nose, 'I don't understand symbols, but I can smell a rat.' " Rosina concluded, "But I believe that Marguerite did not know how to smell perfectly. Gibran is really a refined and noble prince."

The time arrived for Rosina to depart. She put on her shawl, carrying the traveling provisions under her arm, and we left for the Lyons station. On the way I bought her shoes, a dress, and an overcoat. I was sorry that I could not afford to buy her better than a third class ticket. I put in her pocket, in spite of her protests, the money I had left. I helped her find a seat in a comfortable "no-smoking" compartment beside an old woman who was wearing mourning dress and spoke Italian. She was returning from northern France to Rome. I asked her to take care of Rosina. She said, "You had better ask her to take care of me, son." She hugged Rosina with affection.

I bid Rosina farewell and descended to the platform. In a minute the train pulled away. Rosina leaned out of the window waving with one hand and wiping her tears with the other one.

Dear brother Gibran, thus far the one with the golden hair, the companion of Botticelli's soul, has gone with me.